The Trimming o

James Hopper

Alpha Editions

This edition published in 2024

ISBN : 9789362092588

Design and Setting By
Alpha Editions
www.alphaedis.com
Email - info@alphaedis.com

As per information held with us this book is in Public Domain.
This book is a reproduction of an important historical work. Alpha Editions uses the best technology to reproduce historical work in the same manner it was first published to preserve its original nature. Any marks or number seen are left intentionally to preserve its true form.

Contents

CHAPTER I .... - 1 -
CHAPTER II .... - 3 -
CHAPTER III .... - 7 -
CHAPTER IV .... - 11 -
CHAPTER V .... - 14 -
CHAPTER VI .... - 18 -
CHAPTER VII .... - 23 -
CHAPTER VIII .... - 30 -
CHAPTER IX .... - 38 -
CHAPTER X .... - 42 -
CHAPTER XI .... - 46 -
CHAPTER XII .... - 50 -
CHAPTER XIII .... - 55 -
CHAPTER XIV .... - 57 -
CHAPTER XV .... - 62 -
CHAPTER XVI .... - 66 -
CHAPTER XVII .... - 70 -
CHAPTER XVIII .... - 76 -

CHAPTER I

"Why, Goosie, what are you doing?"

Goosie, otherwise Mr. Charles-Norton Sims, dropped his arms hastily down his sides and stood very still, caged in the narrow space between porcelain tub and gleaming towel-rack. The mirror before which he had been performing his morning calisthenics faced him uncompromisingly; it showed him that he was blushing. The sight increased his embarrassment. For a moment panic went bounding and rebounding swiftly in painted contagion from Goosie to the mirror, from the mirror to Goosie; the blush, at first faint on Charles-Norton's brow, flamed, spread over his face, down his neck, fell in cascade along his broad shoulders, and then rippled down his satiny skin clear to the barrier of the swimming trunks tight about his waist. It was some time before he mustered the courage to turn his foolish face toward the door through which had sounded the cooing cry of his little wife.

The door was but a few inches a-jar; it let pass only the round little nose of the round little wife, between two wide-open blue-flowers of eyes. "What are you doing, Goosie?" she repeated in a tone slightly amused but rich with a large tolerance; "what are you doing, Goosie, eh?"

"Nothing, Dolly," he answered, his straight, athletic body a bit gawky with embarrassment; "nothing."

Then, as she peered, still doubtful, through the crack: "It's a new exercise I have—a dandy. See?"

And lamely he placed both his hands beneath his armpits and waved his elbows up and down three times.

"Oh," she said, as if satisfied.

But, as a matter of fact, this was not the accurate repetition of what she had seen. He had been standing before the mirror very straight, then, a-tip-toe, his chest bulging; his arms, bent with hands beneath the shoulders, had been beating up and down with a rapidity that made of them a mere white vibration, their tattoo upon his ribs like the beating of a drum; and suddenly, as if to some singular ecstasy, his head had gone back and out of his rounded mouth there had clarioned a clear cock-a-doo-del-doo-oo, much like that of chanticleer heralding the sun.

"It's fine—it's fine for the pectoral muscles," he went on, more firmly.

"Well," she said charitably, "jump into your bath, quick, dear. Breakfast is ready, and you'll be late at the office again if you don't hurry." She closed the door softly upon him.

It was seldom that she intruded thus upon the mystery of his morning hygienics. It was with a clothed Charles-Norton that she had first fallen in love; and like most women (who, being practical, realize that, since it is dressed, after all, that men go through the world, it is dressed that they must be judged) Dolly appreciated her handsome young husband best in his broad-shouldered sack-coat and well-creased trousers.

Charles-Norton, still rather abashed, dropped into the cold green tub, splashed, rubbed down, dressed, and sat down to breakfast. As he ate his waffles, though, out of the blue breakfast set which Dolly's charming, puzzle-browed economy had managed to extort from the recalcitrant family budget, his usual glowing loquacity of after-the-bath was lacking. His eyes wandered furtively about the little encumbered room; thoughts, visibly, rolled within his head which did not find his lips. And when he bade Dolly good-by, on the fifth-story landing, she missed in his kiss the usual warm linger.

CHAPTER II

When Charles-Norton reached the street, a narrow side-street in which like a glacier the ice of the whole winter was still heaped, a whiff of soft air, perfumed with a suspicion of spring, struck him gently in the face. He drew it in deep within his lungs, and exhaled it in a long sigh. And then he stopped abruptly, and was standing very still, listening; listening to this sigh, to the echo of it still within his consciousness, as if testing it. He shook his head disapprovingly. "Gee," he said; "hope I'm not getting discontented again!"

As if in response, another gentle gust came down the street; he caught it as it came and drew it deep within him. His chest swelled, his eyes brightened. And then suddenly he tensed; he rose a-tip-toe, heels close together, his head went back; his hands stole to his armpits, and his elbows began to wave up and down.

"Good Lord!" he ejaculated, catching himself up sharply; "here goes that darned flapping again!"

He looked up and down the street, assuming a negligent attitude. His forehead was red. "Nope," he said. No one had seen him. "*She* saw me this morning," he thought, and the red of his forehead came down to his cheeks. "It's getting worse; a regular habit. Let me see—two, three; it began three weeks ago——"

He shook his head perplexedly and resumed his way toward the Elevated station.

"It may have been all right when I was a boy," he said to himself as he swung along. "But now!

"Let me see. I was fourteen, the first time."

A picture rose before his eyes. It had happened in a far western land—a land that now remained in his memory as a pool of gold beneath a turquoise sky. He was lying there in the wild oats, upon his back, and above him in the sky a hawk circled free. He watched it long thus, relaxed in a sort of droning somnolence; then suddenly, to a particularly fine spiral of the bird in the air, something like a convulsion had shot through his body, and he had found himself erect, head back and chest forward, his arms flapping——

"'Twas the day before I ran away with the circus," he soliloquized in the midst of the throng milling up the Elevated station stairs. "And later, when I had come back from the circus, I took that long bum on brake-beams. And when I had come back from that, a little later I went off in the forecastle of the 'Tropic Bird' to Tahiti. And each time that flapping business came first. Every time I've done something wild and foolish, I've flapped first like this. First I'd flap, then I'd feel like doing something, I wouldn't know what, then I'd do it—and it would be something foolish——"

The train slid up to the platform; he boarded it and by some miracle found on the bench behind the door of the last car a narrow space in which he squeezed himself.

"I'll have to stop it," he said decisively.

He drew from his breast pocket a note-book and a pencil. Opening the book out across his knees, he bent over it and began to draw. He worked with concentration, but seemingly with little result, for he drew only detached lines. There were spirals, circles, ovals, parabolas; lines that curved upward, broke, and curved again downward, like gothic arches; lines that curved in gentle languor; lines that breathed like the undulations of a peaceful sea; and then just zipping, swift, straight lines that shot up to the upper end of the paper and seemed to continue invisibly toward an altitudinous nowhere. This is all he drew, and yet as he worked there was in his face the set of stubborn purpose, and in his eyes the glow of aspiration. He tried to make each line beautiful and firm and swift and pure. When he succeeded, he felt within him the bubbling of a sweet contentment. This would be followed by dissatisfaction, renewed yearning—and he would begin again.

"By Jove!" he muttered in sudden consternation, straightening away from the book.

And then, "They began at the same time."

And a moment later, "And they are the same."

It had struck him abruptly that the strange urge which made him draw lines was like that which at times convulsed his body into that mysterious manifestation which, for the want of a better word, he called his "flapping." The two things had begun together, and they were of the same essence. The impulse which possessed him as he tried for beauty with paper and pencil was the same which swelled his lungs and his heart, which made him rise a-tip-toe and wave his arms. It came from a feeling of subtle and inexplicable dissatisfaction; it was made of a vague and vast longing. It was the same which, when a boy, had sent him to the brake-beam, the circus, and the sea; it was to be distrusted.

He slammed the book shut and put it in his pocket. "No more of this," he said.

A certain confidence, though, came gradually into his eyes. "After all, these things do not mean much now," he thought. "I was a boy, then, and unhappy. I am a man, now, and happy."

His mind idled back over the two years since his marriage, over the warm coziness of the last two years. What a wife, this little Dolly! What a little swaddler! She wrapped up everything as in cotton—all the asperities of Life, and the asperities of Charles-Norton himself also. Gone for the two years had been the old uncertainties, the vague tumults, the blind surges. Yes, he was happy.

This word happy, for the second time on his tongue, set him a-dreaming. A picture came floating before his eyes. And curiously enough, it was not of Dolly, nor of the padded little flat——

It was of a boy, a boy in blue overalls and cotton shirt, lying on his back amid the wild oats of a golden land, his eyes to the sky, watching up there the free wide circle of a hawk——

"Soy, Mister, wot the deuce do you think you're doing?" shouted a husky and protesting voice in his ear.

And Charles-Norton came back precipitously to the present. By his side a pale youth was squirming indignantly. Charles-Norton's elbow was in the youth's ribs, and his elbow was still stirring with the last oscillation of the movement that had agitated it. "Soy," cried the youth in disgust; "d'yous think you's a chicken?"

"I beg your pardon," said Charles-Norton, in an agony of humility; "I beg your pardon."

But the youth refused to be mollified. Though he said nothing more, he kept upon Charles-Norton the snarl of his pale face and at regular intervals rubbed his ribs as though they pained him exceedingly. Charles-Norton was glad to reach his station.

That morning, in his glass cage, he muddled his columns several times. He was far from an admirable accountant at his best; but this day he was what he termed "the limit." Totals fled him like birds, with a whir of wings. A sun-gleam hypnotized him once, for he did not know how long; and his nose, a little later, followed for several gymnastic minutes the flutter of a white moth.

At lunch, in Konrad's Bakery, he found himself seated, by a singular chance, next to the very same youth whose ribs he had crushed on the Elevated a few hours before. The young man was in more amiable mood. He grinned. "Don't you flap again and spill me coffee, Mr. Chicken," he said, with delicate persiflage.

"I won't," said Charles-Norton. "I'll buy you another cup if I do."

"Got a dollar?" asked the youth, irrelevantly. His thin, pale nose quivered a bit.

"I don't know," said Charles-Norton, hesitatingly. Dollars were big in his budget. "Why?"

The youth drew from a pocket a yellow cardboard. "Got a lottery ticket I want to sell," he said easily. "Little Texas. Hundred Thousand first prize and lots of other prizes. Got to sell it to pay me lunch. Played the ponies yesterday."

Charles-Norton eyed the ticket doubtfully. Usually, he would not have considered the matter a moment. But somehow the incident of the morning had placed him at a disadvantage toward the pale youth. Vaguely he was moved by a wish to regain by some act the respect of this exacting person. He bought the ticket.

"Maybe this was the foolish act that all this flapping announced," he said to himself, once outside, in answer to a not uncertain prick of his marital conscience. "Buying this ticket is like buying a lightning-rod; it may draw off the lightning!"

But his singular malady, during the afternoon, did not disappear. It waxed, in fact; it passed the borders of the spiritual and assumed physical symptoms. "Dolly," he said, when he was again within the warmth of the little flat in the evening; "Dolly, would you mind looking at my shoulders after a while?"

"Why, of course, I'll look at them, Goosie," answered Dolly, immediately alert at the possibility of doing something for the big man; "what is the matter with your shoulders, Goosie?"

"I don't know," he said, sinking a bit wearily into the Morris chair. "They pain; just like rheumatism or growing pain. And they tickle too, Dolly; they tickle all the time." He crossed his arms, raising a hand to each shoulder, and rubbed them with a shiver of delight. "It's a nuisance," he said.

"Well, we'll see about it right away," said Dolly. "Right after supper." Her eyes grew big with concern. "You may have caught cold. Come on, dear," she said, brightening; "I've the dandiest, deliciousest soup, right out of the *Ladies' Home Journal,* for you!"

CHAPTER III

"Why, Goosie; I tell you the lumps are growing. They're great big now, Goosie. Oh, why don't you let me take you to the doctor! I *know* something is the matter!"

Dolly had tears in her eyes almost, and her voice was very dolorous. For the fourteenth time in two weeks, she was treating the singular shoulders of Charles-Norton. He was sitting beneath the glow of the evening lamp, his coat off, his shirt pulled down to his elbows; and she, standing behind the chair, was leaning solicitously over him. A wisp of her hair caressed his right ear, but somehow did not relax his temper. "Well, let them alone, Dolly," he growled; "let them alone. Good Lord, let them alone!"

For two weeks he had been getting more and more peevish. To be sure, for two weeks, daily, his shoulders had been washed and rubbed and massaged and lotioned and parboiled and anointed and fomented and capsicon-plastered, till his very soul was sensitive and a suspicion was agrowl within him—a bad, mean feeling that Dolly was finding a bit, just a bit, of something akin to pleasure in the ardor of her ministrations. Besides, he was fighting a moral fight of his own. Great bursts of dissatisfaction swept through him every day now; and it was only by a constant vigilance that he kept his vagrant elbows close to his ribs.

"Let them be for a while, Dolly," he repeated in gentler tone. "Besides—besides——"

But he left unsaid the thought following the "besides." "Now, dear," said Dolly, kindly, but with a certain firmness; "you've simply got to let me see what I can do. Why, Goosie, you can't go on in this way! You'd be getting humps on your back! No—no; we'll try a nice little ice-pack to-night."

"I don't want any ice-packs!" yelped Charles-Norton (what a bad-mannered young man he had become!); "I'm tired of fomentations and things! Besides"—and this time the besides did not pause, but burst out of him like a stream from a high-pressure hydrant—"besides, it isn't what I want——" And to an irresistible impulse his right hand reached out for a brush and, crossing over to his left shoulder, began rubbing it vigorously.

"Goosie, Goosie, my clothes-brush, my best clothes-brush!"

But the lament in Dolly's voice had little effect upon Charles-Norton. He was brushing himself with grave concentration. "Get the flesh-brush," he mumbled between set teeth, rubbing the while; "Gee, this feels good. Get the pack to-night."

Dolly ran into the bath-room and returned with the flesh-brush; Charles-Norton made an exchange without losing a stroke. "That's something like it," he murmured.

"But, Goosie," began Dolly. Her voice was low now; she stood withdrawn from him as if a bit afraid; her hands were clasped and her lips trembled. "Goosie, dear; don't do that. Oh, don't; you'll hurt yourself. It's getting all red, Goosie. You're rubbing the skin off, I tell you. Why, it's almost bleeding—Goosie, Goosie, stop it, stop it!"

"Feels lots better," he said unfeelingly. "Look at it." And transferring the brush to his left hand, he began to rub the right shoulder, raising his left for Dolly's inspection.

She approached timidly. "You've rubbed all the poor skin off," she announced. "It's bleeding." He felt the light touch of her fingers. "Why, Goosie—there's something—something. Why, Goosie!"

The last was almost a cry, and the silence that followed had an awe-stricken pulse. "What is it?" he asked, still busily brushing.

"Why, there's something"—again he felt the tender touch of her fingers—"there're a lot of little things—a lot of little things pricking right through the skin!"

"Let me rub it some more," he said, transferring the brush. "Now, look at it," he said, after several more vigorous minutes of his strange treatment.

"Goosie!"

This time it was a cry to stab the heart. He dropped the brush and looked up at her. She was pale, and her eyes were very big. "Well, what is the matter now," he asked impatiently.

She came near again, still pale, but with lips tight. "A-ouch!" he yelped.

For with a sudden sharp movement, she had plucked something out of his shoulder. A smart came into his eyes; it was as if a lock of hair had been pulled out by the roots. "Look at this, Goosie," she said with forced calmness, and placed something in his hand.

It was very small and very soft. He dropped his eyes upon it as it lay lightly in his palm. "Good lord!" he ejaculated, his bad humor gone suddenly into a genuine concern; "Good Lord!" he said, rising to his feet in consternation; "it's a; it's a——"

"It's a feather," said Dolly, with sepulchral finality; "it's a feather."

It was a feather—a soft, downy, white, baby feather. Charles-Norton looked at it long, as it lay, shivering slightly, there in his palm. He took it up and passed the luster of it slowly through his fingers. Something like a smile gradually came into his face. He raised the feather against the light of the lamp. His eyes brightened.

"Isn't it pretty, Dolly?" he said. "Isn't it pretty? just look at it. So white, and fresh, and new, and glistening. And see the curve, the slender curve of it—oh, Dolly, isn't it pretty and fine?"

But Dolly, collapsed in a chair, broke out a-crying. "Oh, Goosie, Goosie, what are we going to do now?" she wailed; "what are we to do? O—O——"

"Well," said Charles-Norton, the spirit of contradiction which for several days had been within him rising to his lips; "well, *I* don't see what there is to make so much fuss about. A few feathers are not going to hurt a man, are they? 'Tisn't as if I were insane, or had hydrophobia!"

"But, Goosie, Goosie, *no* one has feathers on his shoulders! No one *ever* had feathers on his shoulders! No other man *in the world* ever did that; none in the world *ever* had feathers on his shoulders that way! Oh, Goosie, Goosie, what shall we do!!!"

"Let them alone," said Charles-Norton, now quite vexed. "They're mine; they don't hurt *you*, do they? Let 'em alone!" He raised his arms and began to slip his shirt up again.

The tears ceased to drip from Dolly's eyes. "You can't do that," she said, a maternal firmness coming into her voice. "Why, Goosie, what would they think of you down at the office?"

"At the office? Why, they won't know it!"

"But *you'll* know it, Goosie. All the time, you'll know it. Goosie, you don't want to be different, do you? You want to be like other men, don't you? You don't want to be *different*?"

This argument had some effect on Charles-Norton. He stood very still, scratching his head pensively. "Well," he said finally, "maybe you're right. Maybe we had better keep them cut short."

"Oh, Goosie!" cried Dolly, joyously, and bounded from the room. She came running back with the scissors. "Come, quick!" she panted. "I'll cut them, short. 'Twon't be much trouble after all, will it? I'll cut them every day. It will be just like shaving—no more trouble than that!"

And she slid the scissors along Charles-Norton's skin with a cold, decisive little zip. He could see her head, cocked a bit side-ways with concentration, reflected in the glass panes of the side-board as she cut and cut, closer and closer. Her rosy nostrils were distended slightly; upon her tight lip the tip of a small white tooth gleamed. A light shiver passed along Charles-Norton's spine. "Gee, I didn't think she could look like this," he thought.

CHAPTER IV

Following this little disturbance the Sims couple, lowering their heads, side by side, resolutely regained the smooth rut of their placid existence. Everything in this world is easier than is imagined. Much easier. In the case of the Sims' household, it was just a matter of adding each morning, to the daily shave of Charles-Norton, another operation quite as facile.

"Dolly," he would call, as soon as his hot towel had removed from his ruddy cheeks the last bubbles of lather.

And Dolly, her hungry little scissors agleam in her hand, trotted in alacriously. She sat Charles-Norton on the edge of the tub and bent over him her happy, humming head. Zip-zip-zip, went the scissors, zip-zip—and a soft white fluff that looked like the stuffing of a pillow (an A-one pillow; not the kind upon which Charles-Norton and Dolly laid their modest heads) eddied slowly to Charles-Norton's feet while he shivered slightly to the coldness of the steel. (Dolly cut very close.)

Then, "All right; all done," she sang, dropping the scissors into the round pocket of her crackling apron; "now to breakfast, quick! And here's a kiss for the good boy."

Placing her red lips upon his, she whisked off to the kitchenette; and Charles-Norton, emerging all dressed a little later, found the cheerful blue ware on the table, and his waffles upon his plate, hot beneath his napkin. After which, stuffing the morning paper into his pocket, he departed with another kiss on the landing, and strode forth for the L. Life was just as before.

And yet, not quite. Because, to tell the truth, Charles-Norton was not absolutely happy.

He could not have told what was the matter. Mostly, it was an emptiness. An emptiness is hard to analyze. He knew that there was much of which he should be content. With the careful repression of the vagaries of his shoulders, there had come to him a new attentiveness at his work. His nose, now, never wandered after passing butterflies, and his salary had been raised to twenty-two dollars a week. Also, the ridiculous flapping had gone, and the impulse to draw fool lines upon a card.

But with these—and that was the trouble—other things had vanished. That deep filling of his lungs with spring, for instance. And the longing that went with it. That was it—the longing. He longed for the longing—if that is comprehensible. He longed vaguely for a longing that had been his, and which was gone. He never saw, now, a land that was as a golden pool beneath a turquoise dome; nor a boy in the wild oats watching a circling hawk.

And there was something else, something more definite. He felt that Dolly—yes, Dolly took too much pleasure, altogether too much pleasure in that clipping business. Of course, the clipping had to be. He knew that. A respectable man can't have feathers on his shoulders. It was necessary. But somehow he would have felt that necessity more, if Dolly had felt it—less. He would have liked a chance to voice it himself. If Dolly, now, only would, some fine morning, say, "Oh, Goosie, let them be to-day; they are so pretty," then he could have answered, very firmly, "No, clip away!" But she never gave him that chance. She was always so radiantly ready! As he watched her head in the mirror, bent upon the busy scissors with an expression of tight determination, a distinct irritation seized him sometimes.

Charles-Norton, in short, was accumulating, drop by drop, a masculine grouch. A grouch deeper than he realized, till that morning.

That morning Dolly, in the midst of the daily operation, paused with scissors in air, a sudden inspiration upon her brow.

"Oh, Goosie," she exclaimed; "How would it be to cauterize them?"

Charles-Norton gave a jump. "Cauterize!" he cried; "cauterize what?"

"Why, the little feathers. Supposing we burned the place, you know, with nitrate of silver, or something like that. They do it to people who have moles—or when they have been bitten by a mad dog. Maybe—maybe it would stop it—altogether."

Charles-Norton looked up at her. Her cheeks were rosy, her eyes were bright; she was excited and pleased with her ingenious idea. A cold wave rose about Charles-Norton and closed over his head. "Say,'" he bawled ungraciously; "what do you take me for! Think I'm made of asbestos?"

Discreet Dolly immediately dropped the subject; though somehow Charles-Norton had the distinct impression that it was only discreetly that she did so, that, in fact, she was not dropping the idea, but merely tucking it away somewhere within the secret hiding-places of her being, for further use. He could still see it, in fact, graven there upon the whiteness of her voluntary little forehead.

He brooded black over it all day. He brooded on other things, too—insignificant things that had happened in the past, that had not mattered one whit then, but which now, beneath his fostering care, began to grow into big, flapping boog-a-boos. And when he returned that night, he was a very mean Charles-Norton. He spoke hardly a word at dinner, pretended he did not like the vanilla custard over which Dolly had toiled all day, her soul aglow with creative delight, sipped but half of his demi-tasse (as though the coffee were bitter, which it wasn't), and went off to bed early with a good-night so frigid that Dolly's little nose tingled for several minutes afterward.

And the next morning, when Dolly, astonished at the delay, finally peeped into the bath-room, scissors in hand, she found Charles-Norton fully dressed, his coat on.

"Why, Goosie," she said in surprise; "I haven't clipped you yet!"

"No?" he growled enigmatically.

"Take off your coat, dearie," she went on.

"And you're not going to," said Charles-Norton, finishing his statement with complete disregard of hers.

Dolly stood there a moment, looking at him with head slightly cocked to one side. "All right, Goosie," she said cheerily. "Only, don't get mad at poor little me. Come on to breakfast, you big, shaggy bear, you!"

"I don't *want* any breakfast," growled Charles-Norton between closed teeth (as a matter of fact, he did, and a fragrance of waffles from the kitchen was at the moment profoundly agitating the pit of his being). "I don't *want* any breakfast—where's my hat—quick, I'm in a hurry—good-by."

And tossing the hat bellicosely upon his head, he pulled to himself the hall door, swaggered through, and let it slam back on his departing heels, right before the astonished nose of his little wife.

She remained there before this rude door, examining its blank surface with a sort of objective curiosity. At the same time she was listening to the sound of steps gradually diminishing down the five flights. She shook her head; "the bad, bad boy!" she said.

She pivoted with a shrug of the shoulders and went back to the kitchen and sat down at the table, all set for breakfast. She took up her fork and cut off a bit of waffle. She placed it in her mouth. Her eyes went off far away.

It took it a long time, this little piece of waffle, to go down. Lordie, what a tough, resilient, flannelly, bit of waffle this was! Suddenly her head went forward. It lit upon the table, in her hands. A cup of the precious blue ware, dislodged, balanced itself a moment on the edge of the table, then, as if giving up hope, let go and crashed to the floor at her feet in many pieces. She gave it no heed. Her head was in her hands, her hands were on the table, her hair lay like a golden delta among plates and saucers; and the table trembled.

CHAPTER V

Meanwhile Charles-Norton was not having such a good time either. Starting off swaggeringly, he had halted three times on his way to the station, and three times had taken at least two steps back toward the flat which he felt desolate behind him. And now in his glass cage, a weight was at his stomach, a constant weight like an indigestible plum-pudding. At regular intervals, as he bent over his books, he felt his heart descend swiftly to the soles of his feet; he paled at the sight of a telegraph messenger, at the sound of the telephone bell. He had visions of hospitals—of a white cot to which he was brought, a white cot about which grave men stood hopelessly, and on the pillow of which spread a cascade of golden hair. Too imaginative, this Charles-Norton, too imaginative altogether!

He did not know that after a while Dolly had risen, and a bit wearily, with heavy sighs, had washed the dishes; that after this she had put the little flat in order; that during this operation, in spite of her best efforts, she had felt her woe slowly oozing from her; that the provisioning tour in the street and stores gay with gossipy, bargaining young matrons, had almost completed this process; and that a providential peep in a milliner's window, which had suddenly solved for her the harassing problem of the spring hat (she had seen one she liked and with a flash of inspiration had seen how she could make one just like it out of her old straw and some feathers long at the bottom of her trunk) had sent her bounding back up her five flights of stairs with a song purring in her heart.

So that when, returning in the evening, Charles-Norton opened the door with bated breath, to find Dolly humming happily in the kitchen, he was struck by something like disappointment. "She's shallow," he thought; "doesn't feel." He did not mean by this, of course, that he wished she had in despair done something catastrophic. He meant merely—well, he did not know what he meant. He was disillusioned, that was all. This was but a prosy world after all. Few Heroics here!

And immediately a warning knocked at his consciousness. He must be careful if he were to hold what advantage he had gained in the day. He turned from the kitchen threshold and silently slunk back into the room which was both dining and sitting-room, and isolated himself behind the spread pages of the evening paper. He was curt and cold the entire evening. And in the morning he again left with calculated violence—breakfastless and unsheared.

This time, Dolly did not weep. She sat long on the edge of her bed, thinking silently; then a silver rocket of sound broke the sepulchral quiet of the flat. Dolly had had a vision of what must inevitably happen; and Dolly was laughing.

It took just ten days to happen—ten days which were rather disagreeable, of course, but which Dolly, sure of the trumps in her little hands, bore with jolly fortitude. All that time, Charles-Norton glowered constantly. He was monosyllabic and ostentatiously unhappy. This more than was necessary, and very deliberate. It had to be deliberate; for, as a matter of fact, on the outside Charles was not having at all a bad time.

The exaltation of the ante-clipping days had returned—returned heightened, and was still growing day by day. A constant joyous babbling, as of some inexhaustible spring, lay at the bottom of his soul. His senses were singularly acute. He thrilled to a leaf, to a bud, to a patch of blue sky; and the thrill remained long, a profound satisfaction within him, after the stimulant had gone. With the resolution of a roué plunging back into his vice after an enforced vacation, he had brought a large sketch book; and he passed much time drawing lines into it—rapid beauty streaks that gave him a sensation of birds. He saw often, now, a land which was as a pool of gold beneath a turquoise sky; and a boy in the wild oats watching a circling hawk. At such times his lungs filled deep with the spring, and his arms were apt to beat at his sides in rapid tattoo. This, in fact made up solely his morning exercises now. Standing with legs close together, a-tip-toe, head back and chest forward, placing his hands beneath his shoulders he waved his arms up and down in a beat that rose in fervid crescendo, till his eyes closed and there went through him a soaring ecstasy that threatened at times to lift him from the floor.

All this, of course, was not without its disadvantage. Vaguely he felt that in some subtle way he was gaining the disapproval of his fellows. Men were apt to look at him askance, half doubtful, half-indignant. They tread on his toes in the Elevated. His work, too, was going to pot; he could not stick to his figures. His chief, an old fragile-necked book-keeper, had spoken to him once.

"Mr. Sims," he had said, after a preliminary little cough; "Mr. Sims, you ought to take care of your health. You are not well."

"Oh, yes I am," answered Charles-Norton, absent-mindedly. His eyes were on the ceiling, where a fly was buzzing. "I'm all right!"

"You should—er—you should consult—a specialist, Mr. Sims. Don't you know—your shoulders, your back—you should consult a spine-specialist, Mr. Sims."

"Oh, that's all right," said Charles-Norton, easily. "Don't worry." And thus he had sent back the old gentleman baffled to his high stool.

And then came Dolly's day.

"Dolly! Dolly! Dolly!"

It was morning, before breakfast. Charles-Norton was in the bedroom; Dolly was setting the table in the living-room. She paused, and stood very still, while a little knowing smile parted her lips.

"Dolly! Dolly! Dolly!" Again came the call, unmistakable, music to Dolly's ear. She tip-toed to the door. From within sounded a threshing noise, as of a whale caught in shallows. "Yes. What is it?" she called back melodiously, mastering her desire to rush in.

"Come here, Dolly," said the male voice. "Come here."

"I'm coming," said Dolly, and went in with a slightly bored expression.

"Help me, Dolly," said the perspiring and be-ruffled gentleman within. "I can't—can't—get my coat on."

"Why, Goosie; of course I'll help you."

But the help, although almost sincere, was powerless. The coat would not go on. The sleeves rose to the elbows smoothly, half way to the shoulders with more effort—but here they stuck, refusing to slide over the top of the shoulders. On each side of the spine, almost cracking the shirt, a protuberance bulged which the coat could not leap.

He stood there puffing, his hair mussed up, his eyes wrathful. "Well," he growled at length; "why don't you go get your scissors."

"Shall I?" she said doubtfully—and at the same time bounced out like a little rabbit. "Take off your shirt, Goosie," she said, returning with the gleaming instruments, now symbolical of her superior common-sense.

She aided him. She took off his collar and tie, unfastened the buttons, and then she was tugging at the shirt. It slid down, uncovering the shoulders. There was a dry, crackling sound, as of a fan stretched open—and Dolly sat down on the floor. "Oh-oh-oh," she cried, "Go-oo-oo-ssie-ie!"

He stood there, looking out of the corner of his eye at his reflection in the mirror, red-faced and very much abashed. For with the slipping of the shirt, on his shoulders there had sprung, with the movement of a released jack-in-the-box, two vibrant white things.

Two gleaming, lustrous, white things that were——

"They're wings," said Dolly, still on the floor. "*They are wings*," she repeated, in the tone of one saying, *He is dead.* "Now, Goosie, you *have* done it!"

But a change had come in Charles-Norton. The blush had left his brow, the foolish expression his face; he was pivoting before the mirror like a woman with a new bonnet.

"I *like* them," he said.

And then, "Just look at them, Dolly. Just look at the curve of them. Isn't it a beautiful curve! And the whiteness of them, Dolly—like a baby's soul. And how downy—soft like you, Dolly. Look at them gleam. And they move, Dolly, they move! Dolly, oh, look!"

The wings were gently breathing; their slender tips struck his waist at each oscillation. The movement quickened, became a beat, a rapid palpitation. A soft whirring sound filled the room; the newspaper on the bed, dislodged, eddied to the floor; the wings were a mere white blur. Suddenly Charles-Norton's feet left the floor, and he rose slowly into the air. "Look, look, Dolly," he cried, as he went up, hovering above her up-tilted nose and her wide eyes, as she sat there, paralyzed, upon the ground; "Dolly, look!"

The humming sound took a higher note; a picture crashed down; the room was a small cyclone. "Dolly, watch me; look!"

And with a sudden leap, Charles-Norton slanted up toward the ceiling and lit, seated, on the edge of the shelf that went along the four walls. "Look," he said with triumph, balancing smilingly on his perch.

But immediately his expression changed to one of concern, and he sprang down quickly and quietly. Dolly was now stretched full-length along the carpet; her face was in her arms. He turned it to the light. Her eyes were closed.

Dolly had fainted.

CHAPTER VI

A husband who has a wife that faints is in the grasp of the great It.

Full of fear, pity, remorse, and self-hatred, Charles-Norton danced about helplessly for several minutes, sprinkling water upon Dolly's brow (much of it went down her neck); trying to pour bad whiskey between her pearly teeth; calling himself names; chafing her hands, promising to be good, to do always what she wanted; loosening her garments; proclaiming the fact that he was a brute, she an angel—while the wings, loose down his back, flapped after him in long, mournful gestures. And when finally, from the couch upon which he had drawn her, Dolly opened upon him her blue eyes, humid as twin stars at dawn, he placed her little scissors in her hand, and with head bowed low, in an ecstatic agony of self-renunciation bade her do her duty. The little scissors could not do it this time, though. It took the shears.

After which there were a mingling of tears, murmurings, embraces, and Dolly said that the bad, bad times were all over now, and he agreed that they could never come again; and she said they would be happy ever afterward, and he agreed they should be happy always. Then Dolly, still a bit languid, in a voice still a bit doleful, drove him off to the office.

Where he arrived very late, and had to pass the gauntlet of his chiefs frigid ignoring of the dereliction.

When Charles-Norton had gone, Dolly suddenly sat up with a click of small heels upon the floor. She remained thus some time, a frown between her eyes. She was not triumphant, she was worried. She seemed to recognize danger; her transparent nostrils dilated to the smell of powder; and plainly, you could see her steel her being. After a while she nodded to herself, curtly and very decidedly, and went on about her work.

She met Charles-Norton at the door when he returned in the evening. He was somewhat limp after a day of *mea culpas*! and she, a quarter of an hour before the time for his reappearance, had powdered her nose—which, she knew, gave her an expression half amusing, half piteous, just like that of the clown who is playing his tricks at the circus while his little daughter is dying at home. "Hello, Goosie," she said breathlessly (also she had rubbed a trace of rouge under her eyes); "hello, just in time for dinner! Made a fine chocolate cake. Poor dear, you look so tired!"

And after supper, which in spite of Dolly's very ostensible effort at exuberance, was rather silent, for Charles-Norton, with a man's detestation of "scenes," still felt somewhat embarrassed at the happenings of the morning, she drew up the Morris chair to the lamp, sat Charles-Norton in it, and filled his pipe for him. When thus "fixed up comfy," he felt a soft breath upon his neck, and two little hands at his neck-tie. Off came tie and collar, and then the coat, and then the shirt, and then—zip-zip.

"Say, Dolly," he remonstrated mildly; "couldn't you wait till morning?"

"There," she said; "it's almost all done. Just a wee bit more here. There! Now here is a kiss! It didn't hurt, Goosie, did it?"

And Charles-Norton had to concede that it did not hurt. How could he have explained the subtle feeling within him, that sort of swooping descent of his inwards that came with, and the dullness of all things which followed always his shearings?

"No, it didn't hurt," he repeated. But a vague dissatisfaction like a yeast stirred within him, and a flicker,—beaten down immediately, it is true, trampled, smothered,—of revolt.

Calmly, coolly, efficiently, though, Dolly had taken the upper hand. The next morning she sent him sheared to the office; she sent him sheared the same night to bed.

And thus day after day for many days. Every morning Charles-Norton went out to his work full of emptiness (if that phrase is permissible), empty of heart, empty of mind, without a desire, without an anger. The warm June days had come; he had changed his underwear. He felt the season only as a discomfort. The emerald explosions visible at the end of each street as the L train passed along Central Park did not stir him; the tepid airs drifting lazily from the sea, the fragrant whiffs from the depths of the germinating land, passed over him as though he were made of asbestos. An insulation was about him, removing him from all things that thrill, all things that distend; there was no color, no vibration in the world; iridescences had ceased; the chamber of his soul had been painted a dull drab.

He had regained, though, the esteem of his fellows. The subtle and unerring instinct which had made them suspicious in the days of his—misfortune, now in the same inexplicable way told them that he was normal again. They looked at him no longer askance. In fact, they did not look at him at all. They accepted him without question in crush of street and L; gave him his rightful space (nine and a half inches in diameter); trod on his feet only when forced to (by the impulse to obtain a more comfortable position); poked their elbows into his stomach only when necessary (that is, when they had to get out or in ahead of him); and on the whole surrounded him with that indifference which at the bottom is a sort of regard, which means that one conforms, that one's derby, sack-suits, socks and shoes, habits, ideas, morals and religion are just exactly like the derbies, sack-suits, socks and shoes, habits, ideas, morals and religion of everyone else, and hence right. At the office he had regained the appreciation of his chiefs; his salary had been raised to twenty-two dollars and a half a week and his working hours from eight to nine hours. His home life was the standard ideal one. That is, he got up at the same time every morning, left punctually at the same hour, took the L, arrived at the office on the minute, worked with his nose close to the ruled pages, steadily, without a distraction, till 12.30, had his macaroon tart and cup of coffee at Konrad's Bakery, smoked his five-cent cigar in the nearby square till 1.30, worked again till 5.30, returned home on the L, pressed tight like a lamb on the way to the packing-house, had a cozy little dinner upon which Dolly had spent all her ingenuity, smoked his pipe in the Morris chair, and then read the paper till the sudden contact of his chin with his chest and Dolly's amused warning sent him off to bed. A very moral, regular, exemplary existence. Dolly was very happy.

And then, just as this couple could see the track clear ahead, stretching smooth and nickel-plated to infinity, an ugly complication began to worm itself into the serenity of their lives.

This complication arose from the fact that the suppressed wings of Charles-Norton began to grow faster. Each day, now, Charles-Norton, returning home, brought with him to Dolly a task more serious and considerable. She had long ago discarded the little scissors and used special shears made to cut heavy cardboard; and she finished off with a safety razor.

The result of this increase in the rate of winged growth was that, whereas Charles-Norton every morning left home placid and docile, his character gradually changed during the day. Starting at his work in the spirit of a blind horse at the mill, by ten o'clock he was apt to find himself, pen-holder in mouth, nose up in the air, following the evolutions of a buzzing flylet. By eleven o'clock, the cage had become very stuffy; spasmodic intakes swelled his chest, ghost longings stirred within him. When he got out at 12.30 the sun seemed to pour right through his skin, into the drab chamber of his soul, gilding it. He hurried over his macaroon tart and cup of coffee, and then had three-quarters of an hour left to idle in the square.

He prepared for this gravely, as for a ceremony; first by buying a Pippin. A slender, light-brown Pippin, scientifically sprinkled with golden freckles, for five cents. (A daily Pippin was a recognized item of the family budget; at one time Charles Norton had carried his pipe with him, but Dolly, noticing the doubtful fragrance given by said pipe to the clothes of Charles-Norton, had insisted upon the extravagance of the daily Pippin). Having bought the Pippin, Charles-Norton did not light it right away. Oh, no. He ambled first to the square. He selected his bench carefully—one upon which the sun shone, but shone with a light filtered by the leaves of a low-branching elm. He sat down; he stretched his legs straight before him. Then slowly, with deliberation of movement, he scratched a match. He brought the spluttering end near his nose. The Pippin began to send forth effluvia, an exquisite vapor, faintly-blue. Charles-Norton half closed his eyes; his soul began to purr.

Before him a fountain plashed; about the fountain were red blossoms; the elms rustled gently against the blue sky; through the delicate lace of their leaves the sun eddied down like a very light pollen; and all this, through the Pippin's exquisite atmosphere, was enveloped and smoothed and glazed into a picture—a slightly hazy dream-picture. Charles-Norton stretched his legs still more; his shoulders rose along the sides of his head. He was as at the bottom of the sea—a warm and quiet summer sea. Down through its golden-dusty waters, a streak of sun, polished like a rapier, diagonaled, striking him on the breast; and to its vivifying burn he felt within him his heart expand, as though it would bloom, like the red flowers about the fountain.

Upon the other benches sprawled some of the city's derelicts. The sun was upon them also; they stirred uneasily to its caress, with sighs and groans, their warped bodies, petrified with the winter's long cold, distending slowly in pain. Pale children in their buggies slept with mouths open, gasping like little fish; some played upon the asphalt.

Charles-Norton, by this time, was apt to be far away; far in another land. He lay upon his back and watched a hawk on high.

The sparrows usually brought him back. They played about his feet; they chirped, hopped, and tattled; they peered side-ways at him and gave him jerky nods of greeting. At times one of them, to a sudden inspiration, sprang into the air; with a whir he flashed up to the top of a tree. To the movement, something within Charles-Norton leaped to his throat.

Across the park, gaunt behind the trees, rose the tall steel frame of a new building; and away up at the top of it (which was higher every day) a workingman, on a girder, ate his lunch. Charles-Norton liked this man; a current of comradeship always ran from him to the little figure silhouetted up against the blue. He should have liked to eat his lunch up there, side by side with this man, his legs swinging next to his, with the void beneath. And then, he thought, after lunching, he would like to stand erect, away up there, at the tip edge of one of the projecting beams; to stand there a bit, and then spring off; spring off lightly, and whiz down; down, down, down with outspread arms.

Which was a very foolish thought for a man that worked in a cage to dream. Very foolish, even if the cage were of glass. Just about that time the Pippin went out in a black smolder, and from a nearby church, hidden between great sky-scrapers, a big ding-dong bell said resonantly that it was half-past one.

He returned to the office. Every afternoon, now, was a tingling trial. He worked with head down, sweating with repression. An obsession tormented him. He wanted to walk out of his glass cage. Out, not through the door, but through the glass. Not gently, like Alice going into Wonderland, but with ostentation and violence, with a heralding crash of shattered panes, scandalously. Out of his cage, into the next; out of that, into the next; from one end of the big room, in fact, to the other, crashingly, through cage after cage—and then out upon the street through the plate front. Half-past five finally freed him; and taking his place in a packed herring-box on wheels, he was rolled back to Dolly—and the shearing.

Thus for a while did the young people live securely on a clown's tissue-paper hoop. Then one evening, just as Charles-Norton, after successfully resisting all day his anarchistic glass-smashing impulse, was watching the hands of the clock approach the minute that was to free him, his chief, raising his bald head at the end of his long, thin neck, said casually, "We work all night, to-night, you know, Mr. Sims."

CHAPTER VII

"We work all night to-night, Mr. Sims." It is always with just such a sentence, quiet, drab, and seemingly insignificant, that Mr. Catastrophe introduces himself.

"Yes?" said Charles-Norton, adjusting his neck-tie and looking at the calendar.

He was not surprised, for this happened twice a year. Twice a year, on a day in December and a day in June, a part of the force worked all night to prepare a statistical table for the benefit of the stockholders.

He telephoned to Dolly. Her voice came to him over the wire in a scared little squeak. "Oh, Goosie," she pleaded; "come up before starting in again. I'll let you go off right away. But please come up, please do!"

"Can't," shouted Charles-Norton. "We're allowed only an hour for dinner, and it would take more than that just to go up and back."

"They won't care if you are a little late," suggested Dolly.

"No, can't come up," said Charles-Norton, astonished at his own firmness (it is much easier to be firm over a telephone, anyway). "There's too much to do. I'll be up in the morning, maybe."

"But Goo-oo-sie——"

"Nope. Can't. Good-by, dearie," said Charles-Norton, and hung up the receiver, and with a bad conscience and a soaring heart, went off to dinner. No shearing to-night—gee! He ordered a dinner which made the red-headed waitress gasp. "Must have got a raise, eh?" she diagnosed.

"No, not a raise, not a raise," hummed Charles-Norton; "skip now; I'm hungry."

The night was a long and toilsome one, but an inexhaustible bubble was at the pit of Charles-Norton's being; gradually through the night he felt, beneath his coat, his shoulders deliciously swelling. And when in the morning he stepped out upon the sidewalk, a cry left his lips.

It had showered during the night, and to the rising sun the whole city was glowing as with a golden dew. The air was fresh; Charles-Norton gulped it down. He felt as though a broad river were streaming through him—a clear, cool river. Suddenly, his heels snapped together, his head went back; his hands rose to his armpits and his arms began to vibrate up and down. A policeman came running across the street. "Say, wot de 'ell are you doing?" he bellowed, red-faced and outraged.

"I'm going to breakfast," answered Charles-Norton, cockily.

He went into the bakery, his hat a-tilt, with the air of a conqueror. For he had decided not to go up to the flat, but to breakfast right here and to spend an hour in the square before going back to the glass cage at nine. His chest pouted; his eyes glistened; wine ran in his veins. He ordered ham-and-eggs and hot-cakes. An orgy!

He was eating fast, in a hurry for the Pippin and the loll on the bench, when he felt someone sit down by him. There was a pause; then, "hello, chicken!" piped a thin voice in his ear.

"Hello, Pinny," answered Charles-Norton, even before looking. He had recognized the voice of the pale youth whom he had elbowed on the L a few weeks before, and whom later he had placated here in the bakery.

"S'pose you're a millionaire by this time, chicken," said the youth, jocularly.

"Sure, Pinny," answered Charles-Norton.

"But really, honest, did yuh win anything?" went on Pinny, more seriously.

"Win?" Suddenly Charles-Norton remembered the lottery ticket that he had bought. He had forgotten it completely. "The drawings was three days ago," Pinny was saying; "got 'em here," and out of his pocket he drew a soiled newspaper clipping.

Charles-Norton also was searching his pockets with much contortion; and it was some time before his hand flashed out triumphantly with a piece of dog-eared, yellow cardboard. "Wot's your number?" asked Pinny.

"Nineteen thousand, eight hundred and ninety-seven," Charles-Norton read.

Pinny was perusing the clipping in his hand. "Wot did you say," he piped suddenly; "*wot's* the number?"

"Nineteen thousand, eight hundred and ninety-seven," repeated Charles-Norton.

The pale youth seemed to collapse. His chin went forward on his green tie, his back slid down the back of his chair, his hands dropped limp upon the table. "Well, I'll be eternally dod-gum-good-blasted," he said weakly.

"You've done it," he continued, solemnly; "you've gone and done it." He looked at his clipping again. "Lemme see your ticket," he said. He placed the ticket and the clipping side by side; his stubby, black-fringed finger slid from one to the other.

"You've done it, partner," he repeated, with the same funereal intoning. "Nineteen thousand, eight hundred and ninety-seven! And I've held that ticket in my hands, right in these hands! Eight hundred dollars.—Nineteen thousand, eight hundred and ninety-seven wins eight hundred dollars"—his tongue lingered, as if it tasted it, upon each opulent number—"Eight hundred dollars; that's what you win. And all owing to me, too."

Charles-Norton had forgotten his ham-and-eggs. He took the ticket and the clipping from Pinny's nerveless fingers and compared them. 19897! That was right. He had won eight hundred dollars. "Where do you cash in?" he exclaimed with a sudden ferocity.

"I'll take you to it," murmured Pinny, still in a daze. "Gee—and I had that ticket in this here pair of hands. I'll take yuh to it. It's down town. No trouble getting the money. You'll treat on it, eh? You'll treat, won't yuh?"

His sharp face was almost beneath Charles-Norton's chin; his pale eyes rolled upward wistfully. A sudden gust of pity went through Charles-Norton. "Surely," he said. "Better than that; we'll share." He paused, coughed. A wave of prudence was modifying his impulse—the prudence that inevitably comes with wealth. "I'll give you—I'll give you twenty-five dollars!" he announced.

"Come on!" said Pinny; "come on—we're losing time, eating in this joint. Say, you'll have all you want to eat now, won't yuh—oysters and wine and grape-fruit and everything. And girls, eh? Autos and wine and girls—Gee!" And his eyes remained fixed on the vision of splendor, of the splendor of Charles-Norton, missed so narrowly by himself.

Together they went down to the offices of the Little Texas, where after having been warmly congratulated by an oily man with a diamond stud, and after signing seven feet of documents and testimonials, Charles-Norton was given a long yellow check, which was forthwith photographed, as was also Charles-Norton. Then the fat, oily man, the clerk who had prepared the documents, Pinny, and Charles-Norton went downstairs and, standing up against a polished walnut counter, drank to the long life of the Little Texas and to the success of Charles-Norton. After which the courteous oily man introduced Charles-Norton to the cashier of a bank, where Charles-Norton deposited his check, receiving in return a little yellow deposit-book, and a long green check-book.

With Pinny, Charles-Norton rode back toward the office. They stopped at the square, and stood a while watching the fountain, each a bit uncertain. Finally Pinny put out his hand. "Well, so long, old man," he said; "so long."

"So long," said Charles-Norton, indecisively.

But Pinny still stood there, abashed and uncertain. "You was going to—but you've changed yer mind, I suppose; I suppose you've changed yer mind— You was going to——" His eyes were on the ground; he shuffled one foot gently. "You was going to——"

"Oh, of course!" cried Charles-Norton. "I was going to give you a share of the swag—of course, of course, of course!"

They sat on a bench. Charles-Norton took out of his pocket the long check-book and opened it out, with a little crackling sound, on its first clean page. He took out his fountain pen. "No. 1," he wrote down with great decision. He paused, looking about him for a moment, in enjoyment of this new occupation. "June 19," he wrote on, slowly, languorously. "Pay to the order of," the page said next. "Of *Frank Theodore Pinny*," wrote Charles-Norton. "Dollars," the check said next, at the end of a blank line. Charles-Norton paused, pen poised above paper.

"Twenty-five," he thought. That is what he had promised. "*T-w-e-n-t-y*," he wrote. The pen stopped again, hovering hesitatingly above the paper. "Twenty-five is a whole lot," he thought. "Just for selling a ticket. Just for selling a piece of cardboard!" And eight hundred dollars was not so much, either. An hour before, eight hundred dollars had seemed an immense sum. Now it seemed a modest amount, a very modest amount. And twenty-five, twenty-five to give away—that seemed quite big. "Pay to the order of Frank Theodore Pinny," he re-read, "twenty——"

The pen made a sudden descent. "And no-hundredths," it wrote swiftly.

Charles-Norton signed the check, tore it from the book, folded it, and presented it to Pinny, a bit patronizingly. Pinny stuck it into a side pocket without looking at it. He was standing on one leg and seemed in a hurry to get away. Charles-Norton, suddenly, had the same feeling. The sense of comradeship which had been with them for the last hour had abruptly flown with this passing of money. Each man was embarrassed, as before a stranger. "So long," said Pinny; "so long," said Charles-Norton. Pinny, with averted head, turned and walked away.

Charles-Norton pivoted on his heel, and started for the office, worried suddenly by the thought that he was late. He took three long steps, collided with a sodden old gentleman who was just arising from a bench—and then was standing very still, looking about him as in a daze, unconscious of the mutter of apology which, together with an odor of stale beer, was fermenting beneath his nose. The old gentleman, pursuing a ray of sun, slipped on to a farther bench. But Charles-Norton still stood there, gazing about him in a sort of mild astonishment, as if, while he was not looking, the scene about him had been transformed like so much cardboard scenery.

To the shock of the collision, as to the stroke of a finger upon a chemical beaker the reluctant crystallization abruptly takes place, there had come to Charles-Norton the realization *that he did not have to go to the office.*

He did not have to go to the office! Here, against his heart, represented by three black figures within a little yellow book, was eight hundred dollars, practically eight months' salary, the assurance of eight months almost of independence, of freedom!

"And Dolly?"

You will think, perhaps, that Charles-Norton was seized by an ardent desire immediately to run to Dolly, spring up the five flights of stairs, push open the door, catch her by the waist and, seating her on his knees, to pantingly tell her of the wondrous news? You are mistaken.

For with the vision of Dolly, the thought that irresistibly came to Charles-Norton was——

That he didn't have to go to Dolly.

He didn't have to go to Dolly and be clipped. He didn't have to go to the glass cage, and he didn't have to go to Dolly. The scissors of Dolly.

Charles-Norton, very pale, his long, strong legs trembling beneath him, sank upon the nearest bench, and tried to catch hold of the world again, of the reality of the world. His hands, unconsciously expressing his mental attitude, held the bench's rim tight with white knuckles.

Eight hundred dollars was not so much. Besides, it was only seven hundred and eighty now. And Dolly was a good little wife. A good, faithful, loving little wife. In a few months the money would all be gone if he stopped working. If he went back to the office and worked, the eight hundred (minus twenty) could be kept in the savings bank as a precious resource against ill-luck. And some of it could be used to buy things—furs for Dolly, for instance, brave little Dolly. Her household allowance could be increased a bit—brave, cheerful, careful, economical, busy, loving little Dolly!

In the silence of his cogitation, Charles-Norton suddenly heard with great distinctness a furtive creaking within the shoulders of his coat.

"Dear Little Dolly!" he exclaimed ostentatiously, making a brave effort to keep his eyes upon his beacon.

But right from between his feet a sparrow, like a firecracker exploding, sprang and went whirring up in the sky. Charles-Norton followed it with his eyes as it went winging, winging up in a series of lines, each of which ended in a droop, toward the high sky-scraper. And when his eyes reached, with the bird, the top of the building, they lit upon a cloud, a great white galleon of a cloud which, with all sails set, flanks opulently agleam with the swell of impalpable freights, went sliding by with streaming pennons, toward the West.

And Charles-Norton felt as though he were going to die. A great, sad yearning seemed to split his breast. He rose to his feet, his eyes upon the cloud. A turbulence now churned within him; his shoulders palpitated within their cloth prison (you see, they had not been sheared for a full twenty-four hours); a wave of madness, of daring, of revolt, rose into the head of Charles-Norton. "No, no, no," he growled. "No more, no more, I can't, I can't, no more, no, *no*!"

The last no was as a trumpet note—a defiant negative hurled at the Force of the Universe. And Charles-Norton began to race around the fountain, striking with his right fist his left hand, muttering unintelligible and tremendous protests. You see, his wings had grown altogether too long. He could feel their ligatures reaching like roots to his soul. When, at the end of the third lap, he came to his bench again, his mind was made up. Only details remained to be determined.

And when he rose for the last time from the bench, these were fixed. His appearance was one of great calmness tense above a suppressed ebullition. Before him his programme stretched like a broad, clear road. He followed it.

Firstly he went to the bank and drew out three hundred dollars in cash.

With the roll in his breast-pocket, he walked up Broadway till he came to a Cook's Tourist agency; entering, after a short discussion aided by the perusal of a map, he exchanged part of his roll for a long, green, accordeon-pleated ticket.

Then he went out and bought himself a tawny, creaky suit-case, and then, successively, going from store to store:

Two collars.

A comb.

A neck-tie.

A tooth-brush.

A safety razor.

A little can of tooth-powder.

A shaving brush and a cake of soap.

A cap.

A pair of much abbreviated swimming trunks.

All of which he placed in his new suit-case.

Then after a moment of frowning consideration, he purchased two thick woolen double-blankets which he rolled up and strapped.

After which he boldly strode into the Waldorf-Astoria.

Such affluence, by this time, did his person emanate that four brass-buttoned boys simultaneously sprang to their feet and came running up to him. He waved them aside with a commanding gesture and went into the writing-room.

He opened his check-book. "3," he wrote firmly in the right hand corner. "Pay to the order of," he read; "Dolly Margaret Sims," he wrote, "Four hundred and eighty and no-hundredths dollars."

He signed the check, tore it off, and let the now looted check-book drop negligently to the floor. He placed the folded check in an envelope, wrote a little letter and placed it by the check, sealed the envelope, and wrote upon it,

Mrs. Charles Norton Sims

267 West 129th St.

New York

and rang for a messenger boy, to whom he gave the letter.

Then calling for a taxi-cab, he whizzed away to the Grand Central station.

Ten minutes later, amid a ding-donging of bells and a roaring of steam, a big, luxurious train began to strain at its couplings on its way overland. As it slid slowly out beneath the resonant cupola, Charles-Norton emerged from the rear door and stepped out upon the observation platform.

And there, upon this wide, large platform, which was much like a miniature stage, Charles-Norton appeared for a moment in undignified pantomime. Leaning over the shining rail, chin thrust out, he shook both fists at the receding city, and spit into its face.

CHAPTER VIII

Charles-Norton's letter came to Dolly in the evening, after a day full of worry. It read:

"DEAR DOLLY :—Enclosed is $480. It's for you. I'm going away. I simply can't stand it, that's all. I think I still love you, Dolly, but I can't stand the life. I can't, that's all. I must have, I must have—well, I can't stand that clipping business any longer.

"Please don't grieve. Some day you'll meet a man who is real fond of you and who will make you happy—one that hasn't any wings. There are lots of them.

"Yours always (in thought),
"CHARLES-NORTON."

"P.S.—Please don't feel too bad about this.

"C.N."

At the reading of this tactful epistle, Dolly, of course, immediately burst out into hysterics. These shall remain undescribed here. There is something mysterious about hysteria which paralyzes the pen. Not the least mysterious thing about it is the fact that the word, pronounced in an assembly of men and women, will simultaneously call up haggard lines on the faces of the men and cooing sniggles in the throats of the ladies.

Anyway, poor little Dolly had it bad all that night, and all the next day, and all the next night. By the morning of the second day, it had passed to a lamentable wandering to and fro within the cage-like apartment, with disordered garments and unkempt hair, through which eyes shone with a glint of madness. By the afternoon of the same day, it was taking some interest in its reflection as it passed the several mirrors in its ceaseless pacing. The reflection reminded of Ophelia. Finally, when in the evening it caught itself nibbling cracker and cheese in the upset kitchen, it realized that it needed new stimulus. It telegraphed for Dolly's Boston aunt.

The calculation proved correct. When, twelve hours later, the Boston aunt pressed the button at the landing, she found herself almost immediately tackled around the neck, while a shriek pierced her right ear. This was followed by a palpitant hugging, from the folds of which emerged vague, bubbling sounds. The aunt bore the demonstration with stoicism and with a certain reservation of self. She was very much unlike Dolly—tall and spare, with bushy brows, beneath the deep arcade of which glowed two limpid gray eyes. These eyes, during Dolly's little performance, remained somehow outside of the enveloping flutter. They peered over Dolly's shoulder in an alert examination of the disorder evident within the flat, and in their serene depths a slight will-o'-the-wisp seemed discreetly dancing. When finally Dolly's outburst had moderated, the old lady spoke. "Where is the bath-room?" she said.

Dolly dropped her convulsive hold and drew back a step. "The bath-room!" she exclaimed, her eyes very big; "you want to know where the bath-room is!"

"Yes, the bath," repeated Auntie, as though astonished at the astonishment.

Dolly showed it to her. A calmness had come over her, a calmness of indignation. Auntie gave the bottom of the tub a hurried cleaning, adjusted the faucet to a tepid flow, dropped in the stopper, and sat down on the edge of the porcelain as the water rose within. "I'm going to give you a bath," she announced to Dolly, who stood there petrified with hurt amazement.

And when the tub was full, she rose lightly to her feet and began to take off Dolly's soiled kimono. Dolly, in a daze, felt the garment slip from her, and then slid into the warm, green pool, which closed softly about her neck. "You lie there a while," said Auntie; "I'll come back and give you a shampoo."

And Dolly remained alone in the steaming room. Little by little, to the persistent caress of the warm water, she felt her body relax; she shut her eyes; from beneath the closed lids tears exuded softly; they came freely, without a pang. After a while, even these ceased. From the bedroom came the sound of a bed being rolled, a flapping of sheets, a whirring of blinds. Auntie returned. "Now," she said alacriously.

Dolly's head was being rubbed; a snow-white bubbly mountain was rising upon it, a mountain like an island—that is to say, like that confection known as a floating island; she could feel on her scalp the wise, soothing fingers of her aunt breaking down the resistance of her nerves; her eyes, shut at first merely to keep out the soap, remained closed in semi-ecstasy.

"Now, out you go!" suddenly boomed a voice, as a patter of water descended upon her head; and Dolly stepped out into the vigorous embrace of a turkish towel. It was passing over her body with a firm, rotary motion as of machinery; she swayed within it like a palm in a tempest. It slid up into her hair and finally twisted itself about it in a turban. A fresh night-dress descended about her; "to bed, now," said the voice.

The room was gray and cool within the lowered blinds; passively, Dolly slipped in between the fresh white sheets; her head sank into the crackling pillow. A little sob rose in her throat. "O, Auntie," she said, "O-o-o."

"Not a word now!" the capable lady immediately broke in. "I know all about it. You can tell it to me when you wake up. Go to sleep now."

It was a pleasant sort of violence; as a harness of flowers the obedience of Dolly's childhood slipped again about her. She shut her eyes, then like a puppy-dog snuggling to its mother, turned and dug her round little nose into the pillow. A snifflet of a sigh sounded—and as it sounded became the first long breath of sleep.

The Boston aunt stood some time by the bed, tall and straight like a grenadier on watch. Suddenly she stooped down and placed a kiss upon the curve of cheek emerging from the folds of the pillow. Immediately she was erect again. "Poor darned little girl!" she said.

She paused again, out in the dining-room, her eyes far away. "*He* tried that once on me," she said reminiscently. A gleam of humor lit up her gray eyes. "I fixed him," she said decidedly. And then, with some tenderness: "Poor great big things," she said; "what chance have they against us!"

Upon which she went into the kitchen where lay a pile of viscous dishes, eloquent of the home's demoralization.

When Dolly emerged from her room some twenty-four hours later, her face was pale and her little nose was red, and she seemed a bit dazed.

"Hello, Dolly," said the Boston aunt, looking up and giving the sofa-cushion she was arranging a final thump; "hello, Dolly; come into the kitchen and have some breakfast."

Upon the gas stove she toasted bread and poached two eggs, which she laid before Dolly like two triumphant suns glowing through a fragrant haze of coffee. Dolly successively suppressed the joyous acclaim which instinctively rose from her whole being at the sight; but she ate. Rather mincingly, of course; but still, on the whole, efficiently. At times she closed her eyes, and then from beneath the lowered lids a few tears came gliding without friction. "Now," said the aunt, after the last crumb of toast had disappeared; "let's go into the other room and hear about it."

She led the way into that little room, which was fairly encumbered with coziness. She took one of the rocking-chairs. Dolly sank into the other. By keeping the same rhythm, there was space for both to swing at the same time. Dolly swayed back and forth three times, and then burst into tears. "He has left me, Auntie; Goosie is gone; ooh-ooh!" The aunt's chair ceased rocking with an abruptness that made their knees bump. Dolly's chair stopped; she looked at her aunt in astonishment. Aunt Hester was sitting up very straight. "Do you mean to say," she began, and then paused as though unable to believe the evidence; "do you mean to say," she went on, "do you mean to say, Dolly Sims, that you made me come down all the way from Boston just because Charles-Norton is gone?"

"Why, yes," answered Dolly, petrified. "Why, yes. Isn't that enough; isn't it *enough*? My life is ruined! Ruined! Oo-oo-ooh"—and her eyes, ablaze for an instant, became veiled by a filmy cascade.

"Pooh," said Aunt Hester, decidedly; "pooh. Charles-Norton is gone; well, he'll come back."

"He's not coming back," wailed Dolly, indignantly; "he's *not*! He has dee-s-s-er-ted me!"

"Deserted," jeered Aunt Hester. "Charles-Norton! A fine chance Charles-Norton has to desert you, Dolly! First of all, he couldn't make himself want to, no matter how much he tried. And if he did want to, he couldn't. You wouldn't let him, Dolly!"

"Wouldn't let him! Oh! Do you think, Auntie, that I am so low, so base, so devoid of pride, as to keep a man who———"

"Toot-toot," said Aunt Hester; "toot-toot—you can't help it. Have you ever read that fellow Darwin, Dolly?"

"Darwin," said Dolly, rather astonished at the turn taken by the conversation; "Darwin—did he write 'When Knighthood was in Flower'?"

Aunt Hester opened her mouth like a fish suddenly whisked out of water. She closed it again. By the time she spoke, she had suppressed something. "No, no, Dolly," she said. "*Darwin*, the—well, it doesn't matter. We've been reading him lately, anyway, at the Cooking Club. That chap *knows* things, Dolly. He didn't tell me anything I didn't know ahead myself; but he *explained* lots of things I had found out. You should read him."

"I'll read him, Auntie," said Dolly, with dolorous voice. "I suppose I'll have to read now, or paint china, or do something like that, now that Charles, that Charles, that Charles———"

"Oh, Charles, Charles, Charles," echoed Aunt Hester, but in much different tone; "you'll get your Charles back. Charles-Norton! He has as much chance to escape you—as the earth has to stop whirling around. You baby! Why, you've got all Nature on your side, plotting and scheming for you. *His* dice are loaded; he can't win!"

"Aunty, what *are* you talking about! Here I am, un-unhappy, and needing, needing, needing friendship, and you sit and talk—I don't know what."

"For, what is Charles-Norton?" continued the Boston lady, as though she had not heard Dolly. "What is Charles-Norton? A man. Hence, a clung-to."

"A clung-to!" exclaimed Dolly, a dreadful suspicion beginning to add itself to her greater trouble.

"Just so—a clung-to. And the direct heir of hundreds and hundreds and thousands and thousands of clung-tos. For of the men since the beginning of the world, Dolly, it's only the clung-tos that survived, or rather that had babies that survived——"

"Auntie!" admonished Dolly.

"Certainly," went on Aunt Hester, seemingly misinterpreting Dolly's interruption. "They alone had babies that survived. The babies of the others—well, they starved, or fell into the fire, or were massacred in the wars. So that now there *are* no others. There are only descendants of clung-tos, and hence clung-tos. Charles-Norton, Dolly, is a clung-to!"

"But, Auntie," protested Dolly, "he isn't any horrid such thing. And he's gone, he's gone—and I certainly won't *force* him to——"

"And you, Dolly," pursued Aunt Hester, unruffled, as though a professor addressing a group of freshmen. "And you, Dolly, what are you? A woman. Hence a cling-to."

"A cling-to!" screamed Dolly.

"Certainly. A cling-to. The end of a line of thousands and thousands of cling-tos. For of the women since the beginning of the world, Dolly, which survived? The cling-tos. They alone were able to live, and to have baby-girls who survived—if cling-tos. The others, and the babies of the others, they starved; that's all, Dolly, they starved. No mastodon steak for them, Dolly; no nice wing-bone of ictiosaurus—they starved. So that there are now no others—or mighty few. You, Dolly, being alive and well and a woman, are inevitably a cling-to."

"Auntie! Auntie!" murmured Dolly, puzzled and horrified.

"To recapitulate," Aunt Hester swept on. "To recapitulate: Charles-Norton is a clung-to; you are a cling-to. Neither of you can help him or herself. For it is the very essence of the being of the one to hold, of the other to be held."

"How horrible!" said Dolly, with a shudder.

"In other words, my dears," went on the aunt; "in other words, you are *dreadfully* in love with each other and can't keep apart."

"Love!" moaned Dolly.

"Love," the aunt repeated firmly.

Dolly rocked for a time; tears again were dropping fast from the end of her eye-lashes. "But he *doesn't* love me," she wailed at length. "And he *isn't* a, a—that horrid Chinesy word you call him, and he is gone, gone!"

"Oh, my dear, of course," said Aunt Hester; "of course, things are not quite as simple as I have been describing them. A woman has to use some sense about it these days. This clinging business has become more complicated with civilization. You may have erred in the details. Now, tell me what has happened, all that has happened."

And Dolly, in a rush of words, told the lamentable story of her domestic woe, of her struggle with the wings of Charles-Norton.

Aunt Hester was silent for a time; then she nodded her head affirmatively. "Yes, that's it, my dear," she said. "It is as I suspected. You have been clinging with your eyes shut. And in these perilous times it is necessary to cling with eyes open. You——"

But Dolly had risen to her feet, vibrant. "Do you mean to say," she began, and her voice was very low and tense; "do you mean to say that I should be subjected to living with a man—with a man"—her voice rose—"with a man, Auntie, who has *Wings*?"

"Oh, my dear!" exclaimed Aunt Hester, hastily, "you mistake me. Of *course*, I am not asking *that* of you. But that is not necessary either. The essential—it is to let Charles-Norton *believe* that he has his wings, not that he should have them. And then, my dear, to be frank, to be just, I must say that this seems to me a case for compromise. Yes, dear, you should allow Charles-Norton part of his wings; oh yes, you should really let him have a bit of these wings. And *that* bit, Dolly, if you are the wise and capable little girl I think you can be, you should turn to the advantage, to the preservation, to the prosperity—hem—of the home!"

Dolly sat down, weak and trembling. She was silent for a long time. When she spoke again, it was in a tired voice. "Auntie," she said, "you mean well. I know that you are trying to help me and am very thankful to you. But we have differing views of Life. I am willing to do much for Charles-Norton—Oh, so much! I am willing to meet him half-way, three-quarters of the way, the whole way, on ever so many things, and I have done so. But when it comes to a question, Auntie, of self-respect, of morality, of *Decency*, then, Auntie, never! On that, there can be no compromise. Charles-Norton cannot have wings."

"Oh, very well," said Aunt Hester, plainly nettled; "very well, very well. Then, what are you going to do?"

"Nothing," said Dolly, decidedly. "I will give him up," she said very firmly. "I will give him up," she repeated grandiloquently. "I will give him up," she said a third time—and broke out weeping.

"That," said Aunt Hester, "is what is known as the *grand stunt*, and is rather popular these days. I've seen many try it, and mighty few achieve it. And you, Dolly"—she rose and stood with a hand upon the shaking shoulders beneath her—"and you, you little soft Dolly, why, you are about the last——"

"I shall not lift a finger," interrupted Dolly. "If he, he, he does not love me, I, I shall, not stoop to hold him!"

"Well," said Aunt Hester, briskly, "I am going now. I——"

"Going!" cried Dolly, desolately.

"I am going," repeated Aunt Hester, firmly. "There is nothing I can do here. And there're Earl's socks to be looked after (he is just entering Cambridge, you know), and Ethel's frocks (she's at the High School), and then there is your uncle—suppose he gets it into *his* head to sprout feathers! No, no—I'm going home. *I'm* willing to be what Nature said I had to be. *I* don't take any chances with those new-fangled grand-stunts. Besides, if you are just going to do nothing, why, then, you can do that without me."

And setting her bonnet upon her nice gray hair, Aunt Hester picked up her grip and marched out into the hall.

"Auntie! Auntie!" cried Dolly, running after her.

Aunt Hester stopped at the opened door and turned. She confronted Dolly, and the will-o'-the-wisp was dancing in the profundities of her deep-set eyes. A tenderness came into them; she dropped her grip, seized Dolly, and drew her close.

"Dear little Dolly," she whispered; "you'll do it, don't you fear. You'll bring back your Charles-Norton, you soft little woman, you; you'll get him! And now, kiss me good-by. Write to me—when you decide."

The door closed, and leaning against it, Dolly wept a long time. Then she went within and in a more comfortable position, wept more. She wept for a whole week. And then, suddenly, one afternoon, she stood up in the center of the room and began stamping her foot.

"I won't," she said, with each stamp of the little foot. "I won't, I won't, I won't!"

And saying "I won't," she did. She sat down at the table and on her pale blue letter paper, wrote:

"DEAR AUNTIE:—Yes, you were right, I guess. I *am* a cling-to. I want him. I don't care: he's mine and I *won't* give him up. Tell me how to do it, Auntie, oh, tell me how! Quick, Auntie, quick!"

The answer was not long in coming. "Dearest Little Dolly," wrote Aunt Hester; "of course, I knew you would, and I am glad. As to telling you how—well, that is very simple. Just go to him, Dolly. Go to him (not too soon; wait a while) and just stick around. Your instincts will tell you the rest. Rely on your instincts, Dolly," went on this incorrigible Darwinian. "They are better than your reason, for they are the reason of your mother and grandmother, and all the line of mothers that came before you. *They* had to be right, Dolly, or they wouldn't have been, and then *you* wouldn't be. Go to him, and stick around, and do as you feel like doing. In all probability you'll be nice, and humble, and snuggledy, and warm. And then, make—your arrangements. *He* can't help himself. Nature is on your side. His dice are loaded. Cling, Dolly, cling."

Dolly blushed. "Auntie is horrid," she said. And then, after a while, "But right," she said.

CHAPTER IX

Meanwhile, unaware of this discussion and of this decision, Charles-Norton, inflated with fancied freedom, captain of his soul and master of his Fate, was having a beautiful time.

Tableau:

A meadow by a lake, on the western slope of a high Sierra.

Below, and far to the west, lies a great plain, liquid with distance as though it were a sea of gold. From its nearer edge, the land comes leaping up in wide smooth waves of serried pines, to the meadow. There the pines stop abruptly, in the leaning immobility of a man who has almost trodden upon a flower. From their feet the meadow spreads, fresh and lush, susurant with the hidden flow of a brook, and jeweled here and there with flowers that are like butterflies. It stops, in its turn, before a chute of smooth granite in the form of a bowl. In the curve of the bowl lies a lake—a silvery lake in the depths of which dark blue hues pulse, and over the face of which light zephyrs pass, like painted shivers.

On the other side of the lake, to the east, the land continues to rise, in accelerated assault, first in long lustrous leaps of glacier-polished granite, then in a chaos of dome and spire, and finally breaks up against the sky in a serrated edge like the top-crest of a great wind-flagellated wave which, attacking Heaven, should have been suddenly petrified by a Word.

On the border of the pine-forest, its one door upon the meadow and facing the lake, is a log-cabin.

It is early morning, and the air is crisp and cold. To the left of the cabin, in the dusk of the trees, a fuzzy little donkey stands immobile as if still frozen by the night.

The sun, still behind the high crest to the east, aureoles it with rose; its light passes in a broad sheet athwart the sky, leaving the meadow in a lower darkish plane, as if in the still half-light of a profound sea; it strikes here and there, among the pinnacles, a glacier that scintillates frigidly. To the west, above the plain, which is as yet but an opalescent gray shift, the last star hangs humidly, like a tear at the end of a lash.

The rose halo deepens along the mountain top; the dark-blue dome of the sky fills with a lighter azure; the star swoons, and the sun peers over the crest. It ascends. Its rays plunge into the pool of darkness still upon the meadow;

they pierce it, at first separately as with rapier thrusts, and then finally billow down into it in a cascade of molten gold. The shadows flee; the sunlight strikes the cabin; and Charles-Norton Sims appears at the door.

Immediately, the little donkey, rousing to life, comes braying to him across the green. Charles-Norton gives him a handful of salt, and with a slap sends him off again.

And then he stands in the door-way with arms folded, facing the sun. He is nude—except for the abbreviated swimming-trunks which were his last buy in New York—and to the light his skin, polished like ivory, takes on a warm and subtle glow. From his shoulders there hangs behind him, to his heels, something that might be a cloak, except that it does not cloak him. It does not envelop him; rather does it stand behind him in ornamental background, with a certain sculptural effect. And it is white, a wondrous gleaming white, against which the whiteness of his skin seems rosy. Starting from his shoulders, it goes out and up in gentle undulation to either side, and then descends in two swift slight curves that meet in a gothic tip at his heels. It is in shape like a Greek urn, but has with it a flowing quality—and the whiteness. It is like a Greek urn of pure alabaster that would have turned liquid, and would be pouring down behind him in lustrous cascade.

Charles-Norton steps forward—and suddenly this background, this mantle, this singular ornament, parts in two glistening sections which rise horizontally to either side of him. By Jove, they are wings! The wings of Charles-Norton. They have been growing, since that *coup-de-tête* of his.

He raises them horizontally, and with a dry rustling sound they open out like fans. He waves them gently, up and down; his chest fills, his head goes back; and from his open mouth, as from a clarion, there goes out a great clear cry which, striking the mountain, rebounds along from rock to rock in golden echoes. He rises into the air.

He goes up slowly, in wide, negligent circles, with slow, strong flap of wings, his body, with pointed feet close together, hanging lithe, a warm ivory white between the colder and more radiant whiteness of the wings. He turns and floats above the lake, then, folding his wings, like a white arrow shoots down into the water. A fountain of foaming drops springs toward the sky. Charles-Norton Sims is having his morning bath.

He swims with smooth breast-stroke, his feet and hands below the water, but his wings raised above. Their roots, at his shoulders, cleave the glazed surface like a prow, leaving, behind, a slender wake; they follow above, swinging a bit from side to side, like glorious becalmed sails.

And thus, like a large Nautilus, he drifts to the shore. He emerges, glistening, upon a little beach which curves there like a little moon dropped by a careless Creator; he takes a hop, a skip, and a jump, and lands headlong upon the yellow sand.

He stretches himself taut, his hands, straight above him, clutching the sand, his toes digging into it, and spreads his wings in fans at his sides. The earth is there beneath him, in his embrace; he feels her strength flowing into his veins. The sun is up there, above him; he feels pouring upon him, penetratingly, its hot life. Content croons in his heart.

But after a while, an uneasiness stirs him. He moves vaguely several times, he finally rises to his knees. Oh yes, of course, it is his stomach—the old tyranny. He walks to the cabin, kicks into incandescence the heap of coals in front of the door, and throws a handful of dry brush upon them. He seizes a long pole which is leaning against the façade of the cabin, goes back to the lake, climbs a large bowlder, and sitting himself comfortably in a hollow of it, extends the pole, and drops into the crystalline waters at his feet a bit of red flannel. Immediately there is a small convulsion and he whisks out of the lake a vibrant little object that looks like a fragment of rainbow. He whisks out another, another—twelve in succession. He goes back to the fire with his rainbows.

There, he—fries them; and—eats them.

Upon which he squats contentedly upon the grass, and fills and lights his pipe. He sits there very quietly, his feet drawn up, his wings behind him like a resplendent mantle; he smokes gravely his little black pipe. His eyes are half-closed, watching the hazy blue puffs of the bowl rise toward the turquoise-blue dome of the sky. Far above him, a hawk is circling; to the sight, after a while, a vague melancholy enters his heart, a subtle and inexplicable yearning. He rises slowly to it, his pipe dropping from his loosened lips. He tucks the pipe into his trunks (that is why he wears the trunks); his wings spread out to both sides. He gives a little spring—and is up in the air.

He hovers above the meadow a while, a bit aimlessly, as though waiting for an inspiration, rising, falling, rising with slow strong flap of wing—then suddenly he is off, like a streak, in a whirring diagonal for the high crests. He dwindles, higher and higher, farther and farther, smaller and smaller, till finally he is among the tip-top pinnacles, a mere white palpitation, a snow-flake in the whirl of a capricious wind, a little glistening moth flitting from glacier to glacier as from lily to lily.

Down in the deserted meadow, the little donkey opens his mouth creakingly, and throws forth a lonesome bray.

CHAPTER X

This is what Charles-Norton Sims is doing while his little wife, back in New York, sits desolate in her empty flat.

On the fourth day of his flight, sitting at the wide window of a Pullman which was clicking slowly along a high summit, he had caught between two snow-sheds a rapid glimpse of this nook in the chaos of the World. In a picture flashed clear for a moment to his eyes, he had seen the cabin, the meadow, and the lake; and his heart had given a leap like that of the anchor of a ship which at last has come to port. When, thirty minutes later, the train, now on the down-grade, had slid with set brakes by a little mining-camp huddled at the foot of a great red scar torn in the heart of a slanting pine forest, Charles-Norton, without more ado, had seized his grip and his blankets, and sidling out to the platform, had jumped lightly and neatly to the ground.

When the last gleaming rail of the train had vanished around a bend, Charles-Norton descended to the camp. It was a decrepit camp, the mine having given out. Charles-Norton found the whole population in the general store. It consisted of five men, about which seemed thrown an invisible but heavy cloak of somnolence. They had entered languidly but politely into his plans. The storekeeper had gladly parted with one-third of the comestible stock which was slowly petrifying on shelf and rafter; a little burro, grazing on the dump, had been transformed into a pack-animal; and after standing treat three times around, Charles-Norton, leading by a rope his fuzzy four-footed companion, to a great flapping of amicable sombreros had taken the trail winding toward the high hills.

The little burro, now obscurely melancholic, grazed in the meadow. Within the cabin, depending from the smoke-polished rafters, a sack of flour, a bag of sugar, a ham, and several sides of bacon were strung, while a pyramid of tins leaned against the blackened fireplace. The bunk against the right wall held Charles-Norton's blankets; the one on the left wall was empty. In spite of this empty bunk, which at times yawned with an air of vague reproach, the cabin, with its wide fireplace, in the center of which a rotund kettle hung, with its neatly strung and stacked provisions, had a certain coziness, a sober, sedate expression of assurance for days to come.

And it was a fine life to live.

He would get up early in the morning, and reached the sill of the door with the sun. He would have his swim, his breakfast, and his smoke—and then he was off.

He was off for an all-day winged romp. He made straight for the crest at first and lit upon the tip-top of its highest pinnacle, rising there out of the rocky chaos like an exclamation of gleaming granite. Its top, hollowed by the weathers, made a seat which just fitted him. To the north and to the south, the saw-toothed crest extended for miles to purple disappearances; within its folds, here and there, a glacier scintillated like a jewel. To the west and to the east, the mountain descended; at first in a cataract of polished domes and runs, then in long velvety waves of stirring pines, and finally in pale-yellow foothills, to the plains. These were very far and were elusive of aspect. Sometimes they were as a haze; sometimes like a carpet of twined flowers upon a slowly heaving sea; sometimes they were liquid, and then the one to the east was bluishly white, like milk, the one to the west like pooled molten gold.

Charles-Norton sat here long, his elbow on his knees, his chin in his hand, his wings drooping behind, along the perpendicular smoothness of the rock, and pondered his happiness. A profound satisfaction was within him; it was as if his blood, at last, were flowing submissively along a great cosmic stream, to some eternal behest. After a time, he rose a-tip-toe, like a diver above a gleaming sheet, extended his wings, and sprang.

At first he dropped plumb, into the abyss; then his spread wings caught the air and held his fall. He gave one soft flap, and then another, and rose. He floated upward; he was even with the top of the pinnacle, passed it slowly, saw it beneath his feet, and still, with slow, strong beat of wing, continued ascending. It was joyous work; he rose on powerful pinion; it was as if his head and shoulders continuously were emerging from one layer of the atmosphere into another more fresh and clear and more beautiful; the air streamed along his skin in a clean, cold caress that enveloped his soul. He passed big sad eagles that flew with lowered beaks, their wrinkled and worried eyes upon the peaks below; he laughed, and astounded, they fell off beneath him in vertiginous circles. The earth beneath was like a bowl, a bowl full of plashing sunshine. He kept on up, rising straight in the cold and hollow air, into a great silence, the only sound that of his wings, beating a solemn measure. He looked no longer down, now. Head rearing back, face to the sun, with half-closed eyes he went on up with outspread wings, an ecstasy clutching at his heart; clutching at it, clutching at it, till finally it was too exquisite to bear, and half-swooning, with dangling pinion he let himself swoop back through the dizzy spaces, back to the earth.

Again upon his pinnacle, he lay very still, long, on his back, breathing deeply, while slowly the ecstatic languor left his body. He was a little afraid of this game, this perpendicular assault of infinities, and allowed it to himself only once a day. It was his dissipation; there was something vaguely perilous in the absorption of it. So, having rested now, he betook himself to less audacious pastimes.

He selected a peak some ten miles away, and shot to it in a line which was impeccably straight. Then he repeated the flight, this time in a slight even curve, flowing and smooth as the rise, swell, and gradual fall of a musical chord. The next time, he flew to the peak in a zipping parabola that was as the course of a rocket.

This game was the consummation of the old yearning which, in days gone by, had impelled him to draw lines upon a sheet of paper. Where before, miserably and inadequately, tormented by a sense of impotence, he had drawn with a pencil lines upon paper, he now drew, with his whole gleaming white body, stupendous lines of beauty upon the blue of the sky.

He liked this. He sensed his evolution. He seemed to have within his brain a delicate instrument that recorded the movements of his body. As he cut through the azure, each flown line was deposited within him in a record of beauty. He flew from peak to peak, in lean, sizzling white lines; in shooting diagonals; in gentle floating curves; in zig-zags as of lightning; in rising and drooping lines that hoped and despaired; in soarings that aspired and broke; in arabesques that laughed; in gothic arches that prayed; in large undulations that wept. Sometimes he drew whole edifices—fairy castles, domes, towers, spires—which, once created, went floating off forever on the blue, freighted with their fantastic inhabitants, invisible, impalpable, and imperishable. And always within him was the record of the created thing, the record of created beauty, etched forever in the inner chamber of his soul.

Sometimes he played with his shadow; he tried to lose it. With a sudden bound that was meant to take it unaware, he was off, along the crest, at vertiginous speed. He went on thus, mile after mile; mile after mile, razing the peaks, he passed along the crest like a white thunderbolt, his wings a blur, his body streaming behind like an arrow. His head struck the air, broke it, parted it; it slid along his flanks in a caress that penetrated to his heart. But always beneath him, like a menace in water-depths, springing from peak to peak in huge flaccid leaps, stubborn and black his shadow followed him.

Of all the lines he knew, however, the one that he loved best was the one he drew when returning to the cabin at sunset. He would come to the meadow from the mountains at a high altitude, and then, placing himself carefully above it, he would fold his wings and drop.

He shot down like an arrow, in a long palpitant line, and then, two hundred yards from the sward, opened his wings in an explosion of fluffy whiteness.

Out of this line he obtained a profound sensation of beauty, of beauty in simplicity. It was as though he had drawn a long, slender stalk that opened in a white chalice; as though he had planted a flower, a cosmic flower, there in the bosom of the sky.

In the evening, after his meal and his pipe, he winged away to a last adventure which was as a prayer. Leaving the warm glow of his camp-fire, he soared upward into the violet night. The earth fell away beneath him, a blue blur, a shadow, till finally the shadow itself whelmed in nocturnal profundities, and of the earth there remained nothing but the little fire, the little fire gleaming red in the clearing. He rose. The night accepted him with silence and solemnity, in a velvety envelopment. He rose. The stars, at first, were all above him; gradually new cohorts of them appeared to his right and his left, on all sides; and finally, his fire, down in the clearing, itself become a star, closed a perfect sphere. He was the center of a universe of stars; the soft beating of his wings was as the hushed tolling of their eternities; the rustle of his wings the crackling of their flames. They moved as he moved; always their center, he could not approach them. And thus encircled, sometimes bewildered, he lost his way. He forgot which star was his; seized with sudden fright, he winged one way and another in mad dashes toward cold orbs which fled him.

But always, finally remembering, he could find his way merely by folding his wings.

He folded his wings, and immediately, of all the stars the little winking red one came rushing to him while the others slid by. It came rushing to him fiercely, with a sort of jealous and almost ludicrous haste, its face red with effort. And with it came the earth, a shadow, a fragrance; its warm, sweet breath fanned his cheek. Spreading largely his wings, he lit softly upon the meadow-grass, by the little fire, by the cabin, home for the night.

CHAPTER XI

Man changes. Toward the end of summer, Charles-Norton found himself insensibly altering the glorious routine of his altitudinous existence.

One day he was tempted by the great plain that lay golden in the West. Idly, he let himself float down the mountain sides, in long descending diagonals, and suddenly found himself above a farm in the plain. In the backyard, children were playing; a man was sharpening a plowshare at a wheel, and out of the kitchen-shed there came a clatter of dishes and the voice of a woman in song. Seized by a sudden perverse humor, Charles-Norton swooped into the chicken-yard and snatched a hen which, feeling herself rising in his hand, straightway shut her eyes and died of imagination. A scream rose from the earth, and looking down, Charles-Norton saw the three little children, legs apart, hands behind them, gazing up with white eyes; the man, back to the wheel, had his mouth open, as if inviting his vanishing fowl to drop back into it; and out of the kitchen door a wide woman suddenly popped, her lips working in malediction. His amusement a bit dampened by this consternation and by the unforeseen conduct of the hen, Charles-Norton went winging back, the dead fowl dangling at the end of his arm, to his retreat, and that night, when the pangs of his conscience had somewhat moderated, enjoyed the best dinner he had had for many days.

This incident reawakened in Charles-Norton a certain interest in humankind. He began to visit the Valley more often.

The Valley was some hundred miles south of his meadow. It was a great cleft that split the mountain range from crest to center. Its walls were perpendicular and glacier-polished, and sculptured at the top into smooth domes and fretted spires. Down these sheer walls, here and there, coming to them without suspicion, whole rivers fell—some in rockets of diamonds, others chastely, in thin flight, like shifting and impalpable veils, others in great lustrous columns that struck the rocky bottom with thunderous impact and rebounded high in clouds of pulverized silver.

The Valley seemed full of people. They came in from the West, in stages. They lived in a large structure, at the bottom, which Charles-Norton surmised to be a hotel, and hundreds camped along the banks of the river, which wound light-green through the dark-green meadows. They wandered about incessantly, like ants; most of the time, at the bottom, but a good deal of the time also along the vertical sides, toiling pantingly up narrow trails, laid like the coils of a riata, till they reached points of vantage—domes, pinnacles, heads of falls—whereupon they immediately sat down and devoured sandwiches.

When Charles-Norton had first discovered the Valley, he had fled from it at the sight of human beings. But now, often, a secret impulse urged him to it. He spent days there, crouching upon the top curve of a great half-dome from which he could look down and watch the little beings at their lives—walking about, cooking their meals, eating them, or following the arduous windings of the trails with sweating noses. At night their fires twinkled red; and once, when Charles-Norton, wrapped in the secrecy of the dark, had slowly floated the whole length of the Valley above them, there had come to him, softened and blended by distance, the harmony of their voices in song.

At first, he had felt but disdain for them, but gradually another feeling had come to him, they were so slow, and crawly, and helpless—and yet so indomitable. A vague pity, almost a respect, swelled within him as he watched them panting, and perspiring, and toiling up the slopes, reaching thus with untold effort heights insignificant to him, from which they presently tumbled down again after their inevitable lunch of sandwiches. This new interest expressed itself rudimentarily in a perverse desire to tease them. Yielding to it one afternoon, in broad daylight he sailed the whole length of the Valley, going slowly, resplendent in the sun. He could see the little beings gather in groups, and see the little yellow faces screwed up toward him; and upon the stage, gliding in from the West like a Cinderella coach drawn by six white mice, all the passengers were standing with milling arms. With a few strong beats, he whizzed out of range and returned to his meadow, chuckling.

He was back again the next day, though, and the next; and of evenings he began to hover about the Upper Inn.

The Upper Inn was a little chalet built on the edge of the Valley's northern wall. It crouched there, small as a toy in the chaos of huge domes surrounding it, backed up against a great granite-rooted tamarack as if in fear of the abyss yawning at its feet. From its veranda, a glance fell sheer, along the glacier-polished wall, to the valley floor, three thousand feet below.

Charles-Norton, of evenings, liked to hover in the void in front of the Inn, his head even with the veranda, his body dangling beneath, while he looked through the glass door into the hall within.... Always a red fire glowed there, within a large black fireplace; and about it, men and women, in garments fresh and clean after the day's climbing, sat chatting or reading. Among them was a young woman who interested Charles-Norton. She was slim and very fair, with hair that lay light upon her head as a golden vapor, and she wore upon her shoulders, negligently draped, a scarf within the white shimmer of which a color glowed like a flame. Beside her nearly always hovered a big young fellow, dark and handsome, but who did not seem very happy.

One evening she rose abruptly, and before Charles-Norton could guess her intention, she had opened the door, and was out upon the veranda, gazing toward him with eyes yet blind with the darkness. Charles-Norton did not move. They two remained thus long, she looking straight out into the void, divining perhaps—who knows?—a vague palpitant whiteness, like a soul, out there in the night; he, moving his great wings slowly and softly, while his heart within him thumped loud. Then he let himself sink silently, till beneath the plane of the Inn's floor, circled, and rising again, took a position at the end of the veranda, from which, peering around the corner of the house, he could still observe her.

She stood there, tight against the rail, as though she had brought up abruptly against it, making impetuously for the void. He could see her slight pliant form, silhouetted against the jeweled horizon; upon her shoulders, her scarf floated like a vague phosphorescence, and her face was whitely turned toward the stars. He heard her take a long deep breath of the night, and then her arms went up and out in a vibrant gesture.

She remained thus, a long moment, her eyes toward the stars, her arms toward the stars, and her whole slender body, arched slightly backward, seemed to offer itself to the stars. Then suddenly her head dropped, her arms dropped, and she straightened, leaning against the rail. The door behind had opened and closed again, and upon the veranda, now, was the big loom of another form, a form which carried, at the height of the head, a warm pulsing glow, like the incandescent point of a red-heated poker.

They stood immobile, the two, a long time. She had not stirred since her first start; she remained with her back to the door, her eyes out into the void. Then the point of light on the larger form slid down, till it dangled at the end of what Charles-Norton guessed was an arm, and a low voice toned in the silence. "Why did you leave me?" he said; "why do you always leave me?"

Her voice answered immediately, clear and warm as a red crystal. "Oh, I wanted to say good-by to the stars," she said; "I wanted to say good-by to the stars!"

"And why did you want to say good-by to the stars?" he asked, speaking softly, as to a child.

"Because," she said, "I am leaving them. Because I am leaving the stars."

"And why are you leaving the stars?" he asked, taking a step toward her.

She turned toward him, now, and laid both her hands lightly upon his shoulders. "Because, John, I am going to you," she said; "because, John, I love you."

"Dora!" he cried.

She arrested him with a gesture. "I have loved you long, John," she went on; "I have loved you long—but I have fought it, fought it, fought it, John!"

"And why have you fought it?" he asked, again gently, as to a child.

"Because, John—oh, I don't know. Because, John, there is something within me—which I don't know. Something which yearns, John—for I don't know what. For peaks, John, for skies, for the stars; for—I don't know———"

"Dora, Dora," he said, a bit sadly.

"And so I fought it, John, I fought your love. But it has poured into me, John, as honey fills a chalice; gradually, sweetly, it has filled my veins, my blood, my heart, John. And to-night, John, my whole being was swollen with it, John, with the love of you, John, and I came out to say good-by to the stars———"

"Dora!" he cried again; and this time enveloped her in his arms.

A horrid, impish feeling suddenly pricked Charles-Norton; taking wing he slid along the veranda and seized, as he passed, from the shoulders of the girl, the scarf, from the conceited head of the young man, his derby hat, and flapped off with them in the darkness. The crash of an astonished chair and a faint little cry followed him for a moment, then dropped off behind.

Charles-Norton laughed all the way home. Half-way over he dropped, into the deepest abyss he knew, the derby hat, which arrived at the bottom, no doubt, in very bad condition. But the scarf was still with him as he alighted in the meadow and felt against his hand the humid greeting of Nicodemus, the lonely little donkey.

Across the cabin, as he went to sleep, the empty bunk yawned, somehow, with unusual insistence. "I wonder what Dolly is doing," he said vaguely, as he slid down the slumber-chute.

CHAPTER XII

Dolly was getting along very well, thank you. Mostly, she was reading the papers. For if Charles-Norton thought for a moment that his indiscretions were to go unrecorded, he was very much mistaken.

Cuddled in the big Morris chair of the little flat, a be-ribboned sack loose about her comfortable little body, her head golden in the soft cascade of light falling from the lamp, an open box of candy at her elbow, Dolly was reading the evening paper. It was all about Charles-Norton Sims, the paper, though it did not mention him by name, but variously, according to the temperaments of its correspondents, as a condor, an ichthyosaurus, the moon, an aeroplane, a Japanese fleet, a myth, a cloud, a hallucination, a balloon, and a goose. As she read, she alternately frowned and laughed. Her brows would draw together very seriously, and then suddenly her red lips would part to let through a sparkling rocket of laughter, and then her brows would again knit in concern. The laughter was of triumph at seeing her prophecy come true, for of course, all the time, she had known that Charles-Norton, left alone, would make a fool of himself; the concern was at the thought that, still alone, he would continue to make a fool of himself.

"Well," she said finally, as the paper slipped from her knees to the floor; "well, it's about time I rescued the poor dear. I must go to him."

She sat gazing mentally back over the lonely two months, the period of her existence now about to terminate, and was astonished to find that, after all, it had not been so bad. Ever since the first crisis, ever since she had made up her mind to hold on to Charles-Norton, the worst, somehow, had been over. It had seemed as if, that determination once made, there was little left to worry over, that things could not possibly come out wrong, that the cosmos itself was with her. And so, she had not worried. And she had had a pretty good time; a pretty good time. Better, in fact, in some ways than——

"Sh-sh-sh," she hissed, stilling the thought.

But why was that?

Well, first of all, there had been the engrossing mystery of the spring hat; this, followed by the still more exciting problem of the summer hat; and now she was planning for the fall hat—she had seen the cutest feathery toque, that came low down about her face, pushing to all sides little wisps of golden curls and making her look—well, very nice indeed. Then, of course, there had been less housework, and she had had much more time to herself, more time and more freedom. The acquaintance with Flossie, the young wife of the floor-walker in the flat across the landing, had helped a lot. Together they had plunged deep into the intoxication of the shops. And several times they had gone off, a bit defiantly, on little orgies. They would go to the matinee, and then have a chocolate ice-cream soda at Huyler's, and called that "having a fling." All this, of course, had been impossible when Charles-Norton had been about. But why? Oh, because he worked so hard, and there wasn't much, there wasn't so much——

Dolly paused and blushed. "Oh, that money," she said deprecatingly; "that horrid, horrid mon——"

She rose to her feet to a sudden new thought and went into her room, where from beneath ribbons, stockings, gloves, and theater-programmes, she drew out of a drawer a little yellow book and a longer, more narrow, green one.

When she returned, she was a bit pale, and sank rather limply into her chair. "Ooh," she exclaimed disconsolately; "ooh, now I've *got* to get to him; get to him *soon*!"

Go to him. But where—how—where?

She knew where he was now, it is true—but only relatively. The first report of his antics had come from a little town in the California foothills; the second from a summer resort in a Valley of the Californian Sierra. He was being reported pretty well all over the United States now, but the first news in all probability were the only valuable clew. They were desolately vague though. A man who flies covers much ground. Where did he sleep? Where was his lair—or his nest, rather? It was sleeping, not flying, that he was to be caught. How could she locate him? It would take time, to do this, and money. And the check-book—oh, Lordie, that check-book!

Little Dolly, always at the bottom a pretty level-headed creature, had become wonderfully patient in the past month. Patient with a determination fixed as a star, as a law of Nature; a determination which was stronger far than herself; which was outside herself; which she could feel, almost, a huge pressure behind her, as of great reservoirs filled through trickling æons; and which astonished her. She had written of it, once, to her aunt.

"Dear Dolly," had answered this Darwinian lady; "you are right. It is not of you. It is of all women that have gone before you, of the millions and millions of women who have fought, and plotted, and intrigued in order to keep alive the spark of Life and hand it down to you. It is, Dolly, the Persistence of Woman; the inexorable persistence of Woman, Dolly, holding Man. Holding Man, Dolly, in spite of his superior physical strength, of his superior brutality; holding him through the ages. The terrific persistence of Woman holding

Man, Dolly, Man—the restless, the moody, the incomprehensible; the erratic one, ever dissatisfied, ever bounding to the end of his chain in blind surges toward painted things of the air which *we* know do not exist.

"Oh, no; you cannot help it, dear little Dolly. Cling, Dolly, cling!"

"That's horrid," Dolly had said, when she had finished this epistle.

And then, after a while, but this time with a smile; "how *perfectly* horrid!"

But now, this patience, this persistence, was indeed a precious thing. It enabled her to wait calmly for the turn of chance which would enable her to find Charles-Norton. She read the papers every day. Truth to tell, they promised little help, for by this time they were announcing Charles-Norton simultaneously in New Orleans, Quebec, Key West, and Victoria. Wisely, Dolly had preserved the first clippings. And after all, it was from the papers that was to come the solution. The paper, one morning, after describing appearances of Charles-Norton in Vladivostock, Paris, and Timbuctoo, had slid from her knees to the floor, when her eyes lit upon an advertisement on the up-turned back-page.

BISON BILLIAM

AND

HIS WORLD-RENOWNED WILD-WEST SHOW

PERMANENTLY

NOW

AT THE HIPPODROME

NIGHTLY

* * *

HENRIQUE FARMANO, IN HIS AEROPLANE,

WILL FLY FIFTY FEET!!

"Ooh!" said Dolly, suddenly clapping both her hands to her heart; "ooh, I've got it!"

She sat there, a little weak with excitement, while a rosiness came to her cheeks and a light in her eyes. "Yes," she said at length; "yes; that's it!"

Upon which she dressed very carefully, put on her hat, and went downtown to the Hippodrome.

Once there, she hesitated a moment before the glazed-glass door with its shining brass plate, then knocked like a little mouse. A big bass voice told her to come in.

The owner of the voice was seated at the desk, leaning back in his rolling-chair, a big firecracker of a cigar in the corner of his mouth. His feet were on the desk, and Dolly noticed them first: they were encased in high-heeled boots that seemed very soft and fitted like gloves. A soft, wide-brimmed felt hat sat rakishly upon his head. Hat, cigar, and boots dropped to a simultaneous disappearance. The man rose, and Dolly saw that his hair was very white and long, and cascaded in curls to his shoulders; and that, what with this hair, the little white goatee at the end of his chin, and the long rapier-like mustachios, of the same color, upon his upper lip, he looked like a French musketeer of the seventeenth century. He bowed, sweepingly. Now he was like a Spanish grandee. But the little eyes beneath his bushy eyebrows were blue and shrewd.

Recovering from her first movement of surprise, Dolly made straight for the desk, her eyes set, her lips firm. "Mr. Bison Billiam?" she asked.

He bowed again in assent. "And at your service, madam," he said, and bent his head down toward her in courteous attention.

But at the first rush of words from her, an agitation came over him; his shrewd little eyes flitted here and there about the room as though suspicious. He stopped her with a wide gesture. "Sh-sh," he hissed gently; "this is very important indeed; we must not be overheard. Won't you step into my private office. Do me this favor," he asked, opening a heavily-paneled door behind him.

Dolly had a glimpse of a broad polished mahogany table, of heavy chairs. She went in; he followed her; the door closed.

Fifteen minutes later, she stood again at the outer door, Bison Billiam, knob in hand, arching above her in deferential leave-taking. "I will see to everything," he assured her; "everything. This is certainly most worthy of being looked into. And I shall do it myself. Myself," he repeated, emphasizing the two little syllables as though that fact were of tremendous importance; "myself." He bowed again, to the ground. The door closed.

Dolly, alone on the landing, suddenly slid the length of the hall in an airy jig. "Oh," she said, "we're going to be rich. I'll have a butler; and things!"

"Clang!" went the elevator, stopping at the floor. Dolly abruptly became again a very dignified little lady. Once out on the street, however, she went straightway to the milliner's, where she purchased almost with the last of her bank account the coveted fall hat. It was a furry toque, with a white aigrette; it came down to her ears and made her look like a little Cossack.

CHAPTER XIII

On the other side of the continent, Charles-Norton's retreat began to be haunted.

He was taking his flight above the lake, one morning, in the cool gold of sunrise, when suddenly a suspicion, a vague sensing of peril, passed like a cloud between him and the light. Immediately he let himself eddy to the beach, and there, stretched low along the sand, with craning neck he peered carefully about him.

At first he could see nothing. Twice he half rose to resume his flight, but each time flattened out again to the same subtle sense of presence. And at last, with a thump of his heart, he saw him—on the edge of the meadow, a man upon a horse, in the dusk of the pines.

They stood there, man and beast, framed by the pines, immobile and silent. The horse was a beautiful silken white, with a bridle of twisted rawhide heavily plaqued with silver; the saddle, of high-pommeled Spanish style, was also heavily incrusted; and the man sat it as though he had been poured molten into it. He wore a wide, flapping sombrero, set cavalierly upon long white hair that descended to the shoulders of his fringed buckskin jacket; the belt at his waist drooped loosely to the weight of a great holster, out of which protruded the lustrous butt of a silver-mounted revolver; long gleaming boots rose to his hips, their toes within carved tapaderos, their heels, high to the point of feminity, roweled with long rotary spurs.

They stood there a long time, man and beast, motionless, a sculptured group but for the slight forward pricking of the horse's pointed ears, and the man gazed steadily at Charles-Norton, his eyes shaded by his heavily-buckskinned hand. Charles-Norton, hypnotized, gazed back. There was something about the man, his flaming accouterment, specially about the gesture—the theatric peering from beneath gauntleted hand—which somehow stirred Charles-Norton with a sense of past experience. They gazed thus long at each other in immobility and silence; then suddenly there ran lightly through the meadow the resonance of a champed bit; the horse, rising on his hind legs, pivoted, the man's waist bending pliably to the movement—and they were gone. A soft thudding of hoofs came muffled through the trees; it rose to a flinty clatter, which in its turn diminished, and ceased.

Charles-Norton, after a while, went on with his usual routine. He had his swim, his breakfast, and his pipe. But an uneasiness was with him now; he cast abrupt, suspecting glances about him, about his profaned retreat. And during the day's long flight, something seemed to follow him like an impalpable menace.

When he returned at sundown, the man was again there. This time he was among the rocks overlooking the cabin, and was afoot, his white horse motionless behind him with long bridle dropped to the ground. Charles-Norton watched him from behind a tree. He stood there long, his right hand negligently upon the horse's neck, his left hand shielding his eyes as he looked; and to the posture, somehow, the whole landscape gradually changed its aspect, seemed to take on an air subtly theatrical, the waning sunlight like calcium, the rocks like cardboard, the trees painted. "Where, oh, where have I seen that before?" murmured Charles-Norton, intrigued in the midst of his panic.

The man mounted, the horse came forward, and with a silvery tinkle of spur and bit, they went slowly across the meadow and into the forest, toward the trail that led to the camp.

"*Where* have I seen that geezer before?" murmured Charles-Norton again, as he was going to sleep that night.

The question was to remain unanswered. The man did not appear again. But on the Sunday following, at dusk, as the lake was aflash with leaping trout, Dolly came running to him out of the trees.

CHAPTER XIV

Dolly came suddenly out of the fringe of the trees. It was dusk; the lake was aflash with leaping trout. And she came to him across the darkened meadow like a fawn panting for her retreat. He stood there petrified, but as she neared, felt his arms open in an irresistible and large movement; she nestled within them, her head on his heart.

They stood there long, without speaking a word, in the center of the dusky meadow, by the sparkling lake. Her face was on his breast; his arms were about her, but his eyes were looking straight ahead into the obscurity. He could feel her palpitate softly against him, and a tenderness like a warm pool was collecting in his heart.

"Dolly!" he said at length.

But she did not answer; only pushed farther into his embrace in a blind little snuggling movement like that of a puppy. He dropped his eyes down upon her, slyly. He could see her shoulders, agitated as if she were weeping, and a wisp of her golden hair, and one tip of a rosy ear; and then, nearer, he saw the furry toque with its white aigrette.

"You little Cossack!" he said, a bit huskily.

Again there was a silence; then he felt the vibration of her muffled voice against his chest. "Do you like it?" she asked timidly.

"It's dandy," he said.

The silence that followed was like that of a kitten after a cup of cream. Then the voice sounded again within the depths of his embrace.

"O, Goosie," she sobbed; "I've been so miserable!"

"Poor little girl," he growled, above there in the dark; "poor little girl!"

"All my money is gone, Goosie—and the janitor was impolite and treated me dreadfully, and oh, Goosie, I've had such a terrible time!"

"Yes, yes, yes," he said soothingly (I'll kill that janitor, he thought, gnashing his teeth).

"Goosie," began the voice again; "you won't drive me away, will you? You won't drive me away; I can stay to-night, can't I? It's so dark, and so cold! And in the morning, if you still don't want me, I'll—I'll go away, Goosie. I'll go away and never, never bother you any more, Goosie; never! But let me stay to-night; Goosie, don't drive me away to-night!"

"Good God!" groaned Charles-Norton, horrified at the very possibility, and suddenly overwhelmed by a sense of the enormity of his past conduct. "Good God, Dolly! don't, don't——"

"I can stay—then—to-night?" she asked, with a glimmer of hope, of hope that cannot believe itself. "I can stay to-night, Goosie?"

"Oh, Dolly, you can stay to-night, you can stay to-morrow night, you can stay always, Dolly, poor little Dolly," moaned the agonized Charles-Norton. "We'll stay here, always, together, Dolly. Never will I move from you again, Dolly; Dolly, my little wife, my love, my——"

Dolly snuggled back close. "Oh, Goosie," she said, "if you let me stay, I'll be so good! I won't bother you at all, Goosie. You can do just what you want; I'll let you have—anything! I won't bother you, you won't know I'm here. I'll just hide around and take care of you, Goosie, I'll do *anything*! If only you'll let me stay, Goosie!"

"Come," he said, not daring to give his voice much of a chance; "come; let us go in."

The little nose suddenly popped out like a squirrel's out of its hole. She no longer wept, though he could see a tear still at the end of one of her lashes, agleam in the dark. She raised her head out of his arms and looked about her. "Oh," she cried, "is that your house? What a cute baby-house! It's pretty here, isn't it?"

"It is beautiful!" he said enthusiastically. "We'll be happy here. Come," he said; and very close, her head upon his shoulders, his arm about her waist, they went slowly across the meadow to the cabin.

It was pleasant, somehow, the next morning, to loll about with trailing wings, undesirous of flight. The cabin, the meadow, had taken on a certain intimacy, a coziness; it was pleasant to remain there all day, upon earth, idle-winged.

Charles-Norton had his morning swim alone after vain attempts to entice Dolly, her eyes still full of blue sleep, into the crystal waters. Then he fished from his rock—twice as long as he usually fished. And when he returned with his string of rainbows, Dolly, uncovering the dutch-oven which he had bought on his arrival, but the mystery of which he had never mastered, proudly showed him the cracked golden dome of a swelling loaf of bread. Its warm fragrance mingled with the pungent puffs coming from the curved nozzle of the coffee-pot, set in the glowing coals. He gave her the fish, all cleaned, and rolling them in corn-meal, she laid them delicately in the sizzling frying-pan, each by the side of a marbled strip of bacon.

There was no doubt that this breakfast was an improvement on breakfasts that had gone before. Bread is mighty good when one has not had any for nearly two months; and warm golden bread just out of the oven and made by Dolly is more than mighty good. The coffee had undeniably an aroma that it had not had of past mornings. And as you held up to the light, delicately between thumb and finger, a little trout with crisply-curved tail, and slipped it head first between eager white teeth, your eyes smiled into two other eyes (like blue stars), smiling back at you over just such another troutlet, golden crisp, entering in successive movements between just such eager teeth (small pearly ones, these).

Oh, you Charles-Norton!

He wore a blanket on his back, undulating from his shoulders, over his wings, to the ground. Dolly had put it there, fearing he would catch cold. Now and then, by some reflex action of which Charles-Norton was unconscious, the wings stirred uneasily to the burden and let it slip to the ground, upon which Dolly, springing up with a laugh, quickly replaced it. This happened so often that it became a game.

After breakfast Dolly, instead of throwing the dishes in a shallow spot of the lake, as it was the habit of Master Charles-Norton, placed them in a pot of boiling water, at the bottom of which, with wonder-eyes, he saw them miraculously dissolve to brightness. "You're a genius, Dolly," he said. She laughed, a silver peal that filled the clearing, then, going into the cabin, returned with his pipe all filled. Nicodemus came to them for his salt, then wandered off again. They sat side by side, their backs against the cabin-wall, the meadow before them, sloping to the lake; he smoked, and she was silent. The sun had risen. It inundated the western slopes with a cascade of light; here and there on the crest glaciers flashed signals; far to the west the plain palpitated liquidly; and above, the sky domed very high, a miracle of pellucid azure. A big sigh escaped Charles-Norton, with a blue wafture of smoke. "Isn't this beautiful?" he said; "isn't it beautiful?"

She said nothing, and so he repeated, "Isn't it beautiful?" And then, curious of her silence, he turned to her. She was looking about her, at the trees, at the lake, and the great crags above, and as she looked, with an unconscious movement, she withdrew closer to him. "It's awfully big," she said, and her voice was almost a whisper.

"It's big with beauty," he said. "Look at the lake," he went on, detailing with the pride of a suburban proprietor; "isn't it silvery and fresh and clean!"

"It's cold, isn't it?" said Dolly.

"And the crest up there. Look at it. It is sculptured—domes, spires, castles. And those gothic arches. They are like joined hands; the granite prays. And see the glisten of that glacier in the haze, like a star in the veil of a bride! It's all beautiful!"

"They're terribly big mountains, aren't they?" said Dolly.

"See the plain away down there. It seems to heave slowly, like the flood after the rain had ceased."

"Do people live there?" asked Dolly.

"And the sky; did you ever see such sky! And the meadow here, how fresh and lush; and the pines, and the cabin, and the lake—isn't it all quiet and peaceful?"

She was silent, and after a while he turned to her. A tear was trembling at the end of one of her long lashes. "Goosie," she whispered, and she snuggled up against him; "Goosie, isn't it a bit—lonely here?"

"*We* won't find it lonely," he answered stoutly, and drew her close within his arms.

The day drawled on, slowly and deliciously. "Let's take a little walk," said Dolly, after a while.

"All right," said Charles-Norton, "I guess I still know how. I haven't walked much lately."

"I suppose not," said Dolly, hesitatingly. They were going side by side across the meadow, and Charles-Norton could feel her looking at him out of the corner of her eye. "I suppose—you have been—doing something else."

"Yes," laughed Charles-Norton, flushing a bit; "yes—something else."

Somehow they did not look at each other for a time after that, and walked a bit apart.

They drew together again little by little as they wandered over the clearing, in a close examination of their domain, which Charles-Norton, with his passion for big flights and sweeping outlooks, had up to now neglected. They found a miniature cascade that purled over a mossy log; a cave, so small and clean and regular that it seemed not the work of the big Nature about them, but of delicate, elfin hands; and then, on the edge of forest and grass, a flower, a trembling white chalice upon the virginal bosom of which one small touch of color burned like a flame. And thus, little step after little step, they went from little wonder to little wonder. Dolly liked small things; it was the microscopic aspect of Nature that touched her heart; she had an adjective all her own for such: they were "baby" things—baby flowers, baby brooks, baby stars. This appealed less to Charles-Norton, hungry for big sweeps. And even now, he caught himself yawning once, and casting a look at the crest far away.

In the afternoon, in the full warmth of the clear sun, he inveigled her into the lake for a swim. They splashed in the silver waters like merman and mermaid; and when, after a glistening disappearance within the cabin, Dolly emerged again, she was tucked in a fuzzy bathrobe that made her look like a little bear.

They sat long afterward on a warm slope in the sun. Crickets hopped about them; Charles-Norton at intervals heard by his side Dolly's musical giggle as one of them struck her. A bird on a long twig balanced above them, and for a time a squirrel chattered at them in mock scolding from the top of a pine. Little by little Charles-Norton sank into a profundity of well-being. He could see ahead, now, his life stretching placid and colored, solved at last, with both Dolly and the wings, uniting love and freedom, the ecstasies of flight with the tenderness of home——

"Goosie," said Dolly; "let's go in."

The sun was gone. It had sunk into the plain, far off. "Wait," he whispered, looking toward the crest, inflamed with living light. The peaks gleamed, the domes glowed, the glaciers flashed, the whole sky-line crackled with a great band of color. Then swiftly from the plain a shadow ran up the mountain sides, extinguished, one after the other, peak, and dome, and glacier; it went up toward the clouds with its long swift lope: the clouds became burned rags.

"Let us go in," said Dolly.

"Wait," he said.

The night was pouring in over the crest, filling the meadow, the dome above; a velvety blueness palpitated vaguely about them; a star, as if touched by an unseen torch, suddenly sprang to light.

"Wait," murmured Charles-Norton; "it is beautiful at this hour."

But Dolly pressed against him with a little shiver. "I'm cold, Goosie," she cried; "let us go in."

They rose, went down the slope and across the meadow. Along the grass a frigid little haze was forming; it was true that it was cold. If Charles-Norton had been a practical man he would have observed that for the last two weeks, in fact, the nights had been growing more and more cold—which might have introduced a disturbing factor in his dream of the coming days. But Charles-Norton, as has been seen, was not a practical man.

They sat within, by a glowing fire. "It's nice to be home," said Dolly. "It's fine," said Charles-Norton, stoutly.

CHAPTER XV

For three days Charles-Norton remained on earth sedulously. It was a pleasant earth. They wandered together in the small area about the cabin; they walked, swam, fished, picked flowers, and spent hours concocting, on the fire before the cabin, nice little dishes which they negotiated gourmandly, like children. On the second day Nicodemus, furry and fat with idleness, was saddled, and they three went down the trail toward the camp. Charles-Norton hid on the fringe of the forest while Dolly shopped sagely in the general store, to the general approval of the somnolent inhabitants who, by this time, had diminished to five; and then they returned in the twilight, Nicodemus a bit wistful with the weight of the many useful and good things within his bags. They worked about the cabin the next day, and Dolly performed wonders with burlap and chintz. Curtains draped the three small windows, a carpet spread upon the floor, and on the big tree-trunk which, sawed off evenly in the center of the cabin, served as a table, a shining lamp was set, promising of calm evenings.

"We'll live here forever!" cried Charles-Norton, enthusiastically.

Dolly did not answer; her back was turned and she was busy tacking chintz along one of the bunks.

On the fourth morning Charles-Norton felt a vague hunger which breakfast did not satisfy. It was with him all day as he wandered on the ground, the tips of his long wings stained with grass. It was with him stronger the following morning; and after breakfast, he sprang suddenly into the air. "Look!" he cried to Dolly.

And before her, above the meadow, he went through his flying repertory. He cut clashing diagonals through the air; he rose and fell in undulations like music; he shot about, gleaming white against the blue sky; and finally he came down to her from the very zenith of the dome in a sizzing straight line which opened, almost at her feet, in a white explosion of suddenly extended wings.

"You baby!" said Dolly, as once more he stood before her, panting slightly, and his eyes dilated; "you baby!" she said, indulgently.

Charles-Norton, shifting his position to one foot, scratched his head. Somehow, this was not quite what he had expected. He had thought Dolly more changed about this flying business; and here she seemed—well, not so very much changed. Within him he felt something vaguely bristle. It was still bristling there the next morning, and gave to his voice a certain brusqueness when, kissing Dolly on the forehead after breakfast, he said: "Well, so long, Dolly!"

"So long," he said; and Dolly, from her seat on the sward, saw him leap from her and wing away in powerful flight. He made straight for the crest; she saw him, flitting up there, a little white confetti in the eddy of a breeze. Rising, falling, darting capriciously, he gradually slid off down the range, and was gone.

Dolly rose. The meadow suddenly had become very quiet. A tree, sap-bursting, cracked resoundingly; the sound went through her like a sliver. She stood there, poised as if for flight, feeling upon her from every tree, rock and bush, the hostile eyes of peering things; and she was mighty glad when Nicodemus came running to her resonantly across the clearing, demanding a pancake.

Somehow, Charles-Norton did not enjoy his flight as much as he had expected. He bore with him a vague uneasiness which no amount of speeding could quite lose. He could feel, all the time, Dolly away down there alone in the deserted meadow. He returned much earlier than usual.

Dolly was cooking by the fire in the clearing, and she greeted him cheerfully, without the slightest sign of reproach. After a while, though, he noted upon her right cheek a little smudge. It was shaped like a miniature comet; it was, rather, like the slight sediment left upon a window-pane by a drop of rain. Charles-Norton, determinedly, refused to see it. But it was there all the same.

And it was there the next day when he returned, and the next, and the next. Each night, as he lit again upon earth after his long voyaging of the air, Dolly greeted him with an ostentatious cheerfulness beneath which could be felt something subtly plaintive, and on her cheek—sometimes the right, sometimes the left—always would be the little accusing smudge.

It spoiled his flights. Following the three days spent on earth, the hunger of the spaces had come back to him, gnawing at his vitals; each morning he was leaving earlier, each evening he was returning later. But all the time, in his wildest soarings, there went with him ... a leaden pellet, a little leaden pellet, very stubborn and indissoluble, there in his heart ... the knowledge that, alighting, at the end he would have to face that little black smudge; that he would have to meet Dolly's cheerful greeting with its subtle, plaintive undercurrent, and the faint smudge upon her cheek.

Dolly, as a matter of fact, was not weeping all the time, down there in the meadow. The care of the cabin, the preparation of the meals, gave her each day several hours of humming content; and in the afternoon she would have several good romps with Nicodemus. But there were also heavy hours during which the solitude of the land seemed to draw nigh from all sides; when she panted, almost, to its pressure, and felt very little and miserable indeed. So that Charles-Norton, dropping like an archangel out of the sky, found always upon her cheek the trace of an erasure made completely enough to show a determination to hide tears, but not quite enough to obliterate the determination; and leaving in the morning, he felt her eyes wistful upon him in a humble and unspoken reproach which all day followed him, stubborn as his own shadow, the shadow which he could never escape. He fought well, did Charles-Norton. He tried hard not to see the little black smudge, not to think about it; and above all, not to let her know that he saw it. But all the time the weight was there within him, spoiling his flights.

One morning, seeing in a sudden flash of naïve hope a solution of their problem, he tried to take her with him. Making a sling out of a strip of blanket, he passed it about his waist, sat her in the slack, and rose in the air. Thus, holding her beneath the shadow of his wings as in a swing, he flitted about, above the meadow, rising, chuting down in long, smooth slants, circling, soaring. Once he thought he heard from her a slight suppressed cry, and then, after a while, astonished at her silence, he came down to the shore of the lake.

Her eyes were closed, her cheeks were white, and her hands were cold; and it was only after he had dashed water upon her that she revived.

"Dolly, Dolly," he murmured.

She looked at him, smiling bravely with her white lips. "Goosie, dear," she said, a bit wearily; "Goosie, dear, I can't. I can't dear. I get dizzy. It makes me dreadfully sick."

He stood there on one leg, embarrassed. He wanted to take her in his arms in great tenderness, but was held back by the tenacity of his purpose, by the knowledge of the peril of such a course.

"Go on," said Dolly, finally. "Go, Goosie; go on and fly. I'll stay here. With Nicodemus," she added wistfully.

And Charles-Norton, the brute, still inexorable, flapped his great wings and went away, leaving her there in the meadow alone, with Nicodemus.

But he was to get his punishment. A few days later, returning at night, he found Dolly truly weeping.

She was kneeling by the fire, frying-pan in hand, preparing the evening meal; and at regular intervals two big dew-drops trickled out from her lowered lashes and dropped upon her hand. Charles-Norton, abashed and puzzled, went about a while, making a great show of occupation, and pretending not to see. And then, suddenly, out of the corner of his eyes he noted the rag which she had wrapped about the handle of the frying-pan. It was not the usual rag. It was a filmy thing within which ran a color like a flame. Lordy—it was the scarf which, several weeks before, he had stolen one night from the girl on the veranda, in the inn above the valley, and which he had since forgotten in the clothes-bag that served him as pillow.

He kept a prudent silence, and pretended not to see it, though vaguely tormented by the very menial service to which Dolly successively put that once radiant scarf. And Dolly said not a word about it. She went on with her little housekeeping routine very carefully and submissively, while now and again a tear oozed from her long lashes. But Charles-Norton felt vaguely now that the balance had swung, that he was fighting now at a terrible disadvantage.

CHAPTER XVI

Charles-Norton began to grow peevish.

"Good Lord," he would growl, as he flew along the crest; "why can't she smile once, for a change, as I leave her in the morning; why can't she speed me away with a smile, instead of that look. Why can't she be happy in her own way down there, and let me be happy up here? Why, why, why?"

He was passing just then a deep gorge, blue beneath him. From it his question reascended to him, tenuous and fluttering, like a lost bird on uncertain wings. "Why—why—why?"

"She looks at me—as if I were a murderer. Just because I want to fly. Just because I have wings. Just because everything in me says, Fly! And I have to carry that look around with me all day long, just like a net, just like a net of crape. Dam!"

"Dam!" said the profundities.

Charles-Norton evidently had arrived at the self-pitying stage—which was a bad sign, if he only had known it; which showed a certain weakening of his moral fiber. He fought on, though. Resolutely he continued to refuse to notice the daily little black smudge upon Dolly's cheek. She was more submissive and dolorous than ever. She had made him, with blankets, a union-suit that buttoned ingeniously about the roots of his wings; he put it on every morning, but hid it behind a rock till night as soon as he was out of sight.

But the very elements, the perversity of matter, seemed against Charles-Norton. "There's no more flour, Goosie," said Dolly one morning.

Charles-Norton did not catch the significance of this remark right away. Perched on one foot, just in the act of taking wing, he had become absorbed in the examination of a fluffy and cold little white object which had just then settled upon his nose. He looked at it close as it disappeared between his fingers in a silver trickle. It was a snow-flake. He glanced upward; the sky was very gray.

"Goosie, the flour is gone," repeated Dolly.

Charles-Norton came back to earth. "Well, we'll have to buy some more," he said, again preparing for flight.

Dolly was silent, evidently considering this remark. "Have you—have you any more—money?" she asked at length, hesitatingly.

Charles-Norton dropped his wings. "No," he said. "No, that I haven't—not a cent. It's—it's gone. Have you?"

"*I* haven't any," said Dolly. Her eyes were very big.

Charles-Norton stood there motionless a while, a bit disturbed. Then his lower jaw advanced; he shrugged his shoulders: "Well—I'll see about it; to-morrow," he said airily, and was off.

But he didn't see about anything "to-morrow" or after. He had a fine time that day. A snow-flurry was passing down the Sierra, and he went with it along the crest, mile after mile, to the South, the center of its soft white whirl, its winged tutelary God. When he returned, that night, a snow-carpet extended down from the top of the chain, down the slopes, to the edge of the meadow. Dolly was inside of the cabin, close to the fireplace. "Ooh, Goosie, but it's cold," she cried. "Yes," admitted Charles-Norton; "it is cold." His wings were encased in ice, and he sparkled rosily in the fire's glow.

The next day, though, was warmer; the carpet of snow gradually retreated up the slopes. It remained on the crest, however, frozen and scintillating. It was a world of increased beauty that now spread beneath Charles-Norton. The crest glittered from horizon to horizon; here and there little lakes gleamed like hard diamonds; and lower, the willows in the hollows lay very light, like painted vapor.

The next morning Dolly said: "There's no sugar, Goosie."

"Coffee is better without sugar," said Charles-Norton, sententiously.

For a few days the young couple, with wry faces, drank unsweetened coffee. Then this difficulty disappeared. Taking up the tin before breakfast, Dolly discovered that there was no more coffee.

The last of the canned fruit followed, and the last slice of bacon.

"Thank the Lord we can live on trout," said Charles-Norton, piously.

As if in answer, the next morning, the trout refused to take his bait of red flannel.

Alone there on the shore of the lake, while Dolly waited within the cabin, Charles-Norton passed a bad quarter-of-an-hour. Then he went up the slopes back of the meadow and captured a handful of grasshoppers springing there in the rising sun. The trout took them with gratitude. "Whee!" said Charles-Norton, when at last he had his catch.

And then, to a cold blast from the East, a few days later, the grasshoppers all disappeared. Charles-Norton took his axe, went into the woods, and chopping open mouldy logs, obtained a store of white grub. The trout took them.

But Fatality now was dogging him close. When, with tingling skin, he opened the cabin-door a few mornings later, a cry escaped him. A snow-carpet spread from the crest over the face of the whole visible world, clear down to the western plain. It covered deep the meadow, hung in miniature mountain-chains on the boughs of the pines, filigreed the lake. The lake was frozen.

Charles-Norton chopped a hole in the ice, then chopped logs and replenished his supply of grubs. The trout refused them. They could not be blamed; the grubs, hibernating, had shrunk themselves into hard little sticks devoid of the least suspicion of succulence.

Charles-Norton and Dolly went breakfastless that morning. All day Charles-Norton roamed above the land with a vague idea of catching something. But living creatures seemed to have withdrawn into the earth; the few still out had put on white liveries; when Charles-Norton flew low, they fled him, and when he flew high, he could not distinguish them from the earth's impassive mantle. He thought once of the ranch in the plain and of its chicken-yard, but dropped the idea immediately. Dolly's vigorous little New England conscience would never accept a compromise such as this.

Charles-Norton and Dolly that night went supperless to bed; they arose in the morning with no prospect of breakfast. Charles-Norton moped long at the fire while Dolly, very wisely silent, trotted about her work. Suddenly Charles-Norton rose with a smothered exclamation. In two strides he made for the door, opened it, and took wing; Dolly saw him flitting among the branches of the pines in mysterious occupation. He returned in great triumph and threw on the table a double handful of small, dry objects that looked like wooden beans. "We'll eat pine-nuts!" he cried enthusiastically. "Pine-nuts are just chuck full of protein!"

For three days they lived on pine-nuts. And then, as on the third evening, they sat before the little heap which made their meal, Dolly fell forward on the table with a wide movement of her arms that scattered the supper in a dry tinkle to the floor, and remained thus with heaving shoulders.

Charles-Norton rose and stood above her. Dolly was weeping this time, truly weeping, beyond the slightest doubt, openly and freely. This was the end; he was cornered at last, his last twisting over. She wept there in an abandonment of woe, her face in her arms, her hair desolate on the surface of the table, her shoulders palpitating. And as he gazed down upon her, a great, vague mournfulness slowly rose through him, a mournfulness part regret, part sacrifice; he stood there gazing down upon her as a child gazing down on a broken toy, a broken toy in the ruin of which lay the ruin of his dreams. She wept; and he felt as if a wreath, a wreath soft and flowery but very heavy, had fallen about his neck and were drawing him down, down out of the altitudes of his will. And so, gently, he asked the question, the answer of which he knew, the asking of which was renunciation.

"Dolly, Dolly," he whispered; "what is the matter, Dolly?"

"Ooh, ooh, ooh," sobbed Dolly; "ooh, Goosie, I can't—can't eat pine-nuts, Goosie! I can't!"

Her shoulders shook, the table trembled, her wail rose to a perfect little whistle of woe. Charles-Norton sat down by her and took her in his arms. "Well, we won't have to, Dolly," he said gently; "us won't have to. We—we'll go back!"

They remained thus long, entwined, while little by little the violence of Dolly's despair moderated. At length she freed herself, with a smile like the sunlight of an April shower, and still with a little catch in her throat, took the lamp from the table and set it on the sill of the western window.

Half an hour later there was a knock at the door.

CHAPTER XVII

After a moment of indecision, during which Dolly, rosy with excitement, was hurriedly rearranging her disordered apparel, Charles-Norton, picking up the lamp, strode to the door and opened it. His lips were unable to hold a short exclamation of surprise. For, framed in the door-way, there stood the mysterious stranger whom twice he had caught watching him in the meadow.

He stood there, very tall, soft hat in hand, his white hair and cavalier mustachios shining softly in the rays of the lamp, the fringes of his buckskin garments all aglitter with the cold; above his right shoulder there peered affectionately the white face of his horse, the vague loom of whom could be divined behind in the night. He placed his right foot upon the lintel, and to the movement his long spur tinkled in a single silver note. "May I come in?" he asked gravely.

"Why, yes; why, yes," exclaimed Charles-Norton, recovering from his momentary petrifaction; "come in, make yourself at home, have a chair, have a seat!"

"Back!" said the man, over his shoulder, and to the command the inquisitive nose of the white horse receded in the darkness. The man shut the door, behind which, immediately, a philosophical munching of bit began to sound. He walked across the room with a low bow which caused the wide brim of his hat to sweep the floor; and to Charles-Norton's invitation sat himself on the bench by the fireplace. Dolly perched herself on the side of her bunk, Charles-Norton on his. They formed thus a triangle, of which the stranger was the apex. Dolly's face was flushed, her eyes were bright, but she kept them carefully averted from the gleaming visitor. Charles-Norton, on the contrary, stared at him frankly. A reminiscence was coming slowly, like a light, into his brain.

"I've seen you before," he said. "Twice I've seen you with your horse, here, among the rocks."

"Did you see me?" said the man, with a smile.

"I couldn't place you then. But now I know. I know who you are. You're Bison Billiam, aren't you; Bison Billiam, the great scout."

"So I am popularly known," said the man, with a bow.

"I remember you. It's ten, twelve years ago. You came out of a lot of cardboard scenery at the end of the hall, hunting buffaloes. The calcium light was on you, and you looked like this———"

Here Charles-Norton placed his right hand above his eyes in most approved scouting style, and peered to right and left. "Humph," said Bison Billiam, seemingly not altogether delighted with this representation.

"And you saw the buffalo—three of them—father and mother and son, I guess—standing in the center of the arena. You galloped right into them, and emptied the magazine of your Winchester into them—but they wouldn't run. They knew you too well, I suppose."

"I suppose," agreed Bison Billiam. "The buffaloes I've hunted in the last twenty years have known me pretty well. It was not so once," he said reminiscently; "not so, not so———"

There was a little silence at this evocation of the melancholy of gone days. The fire crackled. It was Bison Billiam who spoke first. "I've been watching you fly," he said.

"Yes?" exclaimed Charles-Norton, flushing with pleasure and doubt.

"I have a permanent show in New York now," went on Bison Billiam.

"Yes?" said Charles-Norton.

"I want you to fly there," said Bison Billiam.

"Yes?" said Charles-Norton.

"I'll give you four hundred a week."

Charles-Norton fell backward into his bunk, his legs swaying perpendicularly in the air like two derricks gone amuck. From the depths of his involuntary position he heard the silvery pealing of Dolly's laughter. When he rose again though, Dolly had ceased laughing, and Bison Billiam's face had a gravity which somehow vaguely impressed Charles-Norton as without solidity, like fresh varnish. The two looked as though they had been gazing at each other, but their eyes now were carefully averted.

"I didn't understand," said Charles-Norton, with dignity, and surreptitiously took a firm hold of the edge of the bunk.

"The matter is simply this," said Bison Billiam. "I have a permanent Wild West show in New York. I want a new feature for it. You are it. I'll give you three hundred a———"

"Four hundred; you said four hundred!" exclaimed Dolly.

He turned to her with a bow which held homage. "Four hundred," he corrected.

"What will I have to do?" asked Charles-Norton, still somewhat dazed.

"Just fly. Fly every night, and at the matinees, Wednesdays and Saturdays. The police will stand for it, I think—except on Sundays. But we'll settle the details later. Meanwhile, here's the contract." He fumbled in the inside of his buckskin jacket and drew out a typewritten document.

Charles-Norton stood long over the contract, spread out on the table. He pretended to read it, but was too agitated to do so. The little purple characters danced in the glow of the lamp. Upon his right shoulder he could feel Dolly's chin; it rested there tenderly, with wistfulness, in prayer. Mixed with his excitement was a vague sadness, a sadness, somehow, as though he were saying farewell to someone. But he had already gone through the crisis; to Dolly's heart-rending cry upon the dietary inadequacy of pine-nuts, he had yielded his whole being in supreme sacrifice. An exultation possessed him at the thought, a madness of self-gift. He straightened to his full height; "I'll sign!" he cried with ringing accent.

He felt Dolly turn about him; she laid her head upon his breast. "Sh-sh, sh-sh," he whispered, patting her; "it's all right, Dolly." He raised his head once more. "I'll sign!" he declared again loudly.

"Well, I should say so," murmured Bison Billiam, a bit amazed at all this ceremony. Out of the holster which hung on his belt, he drew a fountain-pen, which lay snugly by the silver-mounted revolver. And Charles-Norton, his left arm about Dolly, with his right hand signed firmly the contract.

"I'll be back in the morning," said Bison Billiam as he mounted his horse. "You'll give me an exhibition, and we'll settle on your stunt and on the size of your machine—your——"

But his last word flew away with him in the night. Charles-Norton closed the door. There was a little silence. "What did he mean?" asked Charles-Norton; "what did he mean by the size, the size of——"

"Oh, I don't know," said Dolly. "Goosie, you are a dear; a darling, Goosie. Goosie——"

"That's all right, little girl," said Charles-Norton with large magnanimity; "glad to do it for you." And then, nudging Dolly with his elbow, "four hundred a week, Dolly; four hundred! Gee!" he cried.

The practical side of Charles-Norton seemed at last awakened; he danced around the table in glee. But Dolly, singularly, did not join in.

The next morning, bright and early, Dolly and Charles-Norton heard a haloo outside and, emerging, found Bison Billiam erect upon his motionless horse in the center of the snow-covered meadow. "You've had breakfast?" he asked pleasantly.

"Well—yes," said Dolly; "just got through," said the little liar (there wasn't anything within the cabin to breakfast upon).

"We'll begin right away, then," said Bison Billiam. "We leave at noon."

He dismounted, and Dolly and he seated themselves side by side, with backs against the cabin, while Charles-Norton gave them an exhibition.

He winged off first directly for the crest gleaming high in the distance, making his line straight and swift; then returned in a perfect curve that spanned the distance like a rainbow. Remaining above the meadow, now, he drew all his fantasies against the sky and finally, rising high till he was a mere dot in the heavens, he shot down like a white thunderbolt and landed at their feet in snowy explosion of extended wings.

He found Bison Billiam and Dolly conferring earnestly. "Two feet, I think," Bison Billiam said. Dolly ran into the cabin and returned with a pair of glittering scissors.

"What are you going to do?" asked Charles-Norton, suddenly cold and distrustful.

"Cut off two feet," said Dolly, laughingly. "Mr. Billiam says to cut off two feet."

"Off my wings?" yelped Charles-Norton; "off my wings?"

Dolly turned her eyes to Bison Billiam in doubt, in appeal. "It's in the contract, young man," said Bison Billiam. "Haven't you read the contract?" he said, drawing the document from his jacket.

"No, I haven't," said Charles-Norton, shortly. "Let me see it."

And he read, beneath Bison Billiam's pointing finger: "It shall be regarded as a part of this agreement that the length of the flying apparatus, whatsoever it may be, shall be determined by the party of the first part."

"I won't!" thundered Charles-Norton.

"Goosie, dear," implored Dolly; "Goosie, dear, only two feet, and it's in the contract, Goosie, dear——"

He turned upon her fiercely. "Why can't you eat pine-nuts?" he cried; "why, why, why?"

She drew back a step and looked at him with great large eyes, and as he met them, he saw them fill slowly with tears. "I can't," she said simply; "I can't, Goosie." Again Charles-Norton had that sensation of a wreath falling about his neck, a heavy wreath within the soft flowers of which was hidden a good stout chain. "All right; go ahead," he said, with a sigh.

Dolly, with the firmness of a surgeon inexorably sure of what is best for his patient, curtailed the "flying apparatus" to the required length. "Now, let's see you," said Bison Billiam.

And Charles-Norton repeated his performance, more heavily this time, in smaller compass. But when he descended, again he was met by Bison Billiam's disapproving head-shake. "We'll have to take off another foot," said Bison Billiam.

"But why?" remonstrated Charles-Norton (with the first cut there had already come to him a certain lassitude, an indifference, almost, which made him much more tractable). "Why do you want my wings short?" (also he was conscious of a feeling of aspiration amidships, of aspiration for something else than pine-nuts). "Don't you want me to fly well? What the deuce is the matter?"

"It won't do; it won't do at all," said Bison Billiam, in a tone almost of discouragement. "Can't you *see* it won't do?" he went on impatiently. "It's too smooth; there's no effort in it. Lord, you do it as though it were *easy*! And there's no *danger* in it, man! Lord, I sit here and watch you without batting an eye-lid; feeling sure you can't fall. That's not what I want. I want the audience to get excited, to palpitate! I don't want them to sit there like lambs watching a cloud, or a bird flying. Your act isn't worth two-bits a week. I want men to groan, children to scream, women to faint! Lop 'em off!"

Again Charles-Norton submitted himself to Dolly's gentle fingers and cold scissors, and repeated his act with shortened wings. This happened three times. Three times the scissors zipped, down eddied to the ground, and Charles-Norton tried again, more heavily, more soddenly, his being invaded by the emptiness of the old days, the shorn days.

At the end of the third flight, Bison Billiam remained silent a long time, evidently the prey of a heavy discouragement. Suddenly the light of inspiration sprang to his brow; his voice rang clear in the glade. "Cut six inches off the left wing," he cried, "and leave the right as it is. Shear the left and leave the right as it is!"

Charles-Norton gazed at him open-mouthed. But by this time there was little left in him strong enough for rebellion. He closed his mouth again. Dolly interceded with a glance of her soft eyes, but Bison Billiam was aglow with his idea. "Cut!" he cried.

Dolly cut.

This time the result was eminently satisfactory. With great effort, with cracking sinew and sweating brow, Charles-Norton managed to circle the meadow once with heavy, awkward flapping. His neck was awry with the uneven pressure, his fine body was twisted; he almost struck the ground between each stroke, and as he was passing his audience on the beginning of a second lap, he lost control suddenly, turned clear over, and flopped to earth at their feet.

Bison Billiam could not restrain his enthusiasm now. He clapped his hands, he skipped about like a child. "Fine; fine!" he cried, and his deep voice rang clear to the crest; "that's the stuff; now we've got it! By Jove," he swore, his satisfaction rising to delirium, "I'll give you four hundred *and fifty* a week!"

They left immediately, Charles-Norton dressing, for the first time in many days, in his city suit of clothes. The wings, even though—rectified, bulged the coat, but this was hidden by the cape of his mackintosh, which Dolly, providentially, had brought with her from the city. They wended their way back along the trail to the camp, Charles-Norton bronzed like a farmer, choking in his white collar, Dolly very pretty in her tailor suit, her furs, and her toque, Bison Billiam resplendent on his white horse; and before them Nicodemus trotted demurely, a dress-suit case in each saddle-bag, another slung atop. They left him at the camp, grazing philosophically on his old dump. Charles-Norton gave him an affectionate farewell slap, Dolly kissed him on the nose, and they then climbed aboard the shining private-car which stood ready for them on the siding. One end of the private-car was a luxurious stable, in which the white horse climbed along a cleated gang-way. A half-hour later the passing Overland train picked up the car, and slowly clicking along the summit, they saw, between two snow-sheds, the little meadow, its lake, and its cabin, pass by, out of their vision, out of their lives.

Charles-Norton took off his coat, which felt very tight. A private-car had a freedom, and comforts, which a public-car has not; a faint appreciation of this fact came to Charles-Norton as he settled back, coatless, in his upholstered chair, and with it the first vague snuggle of readjustment. This feeling became clearer after the dainty breakfast served by Bison Billiam's white-capped cook, and expressed itself in a sigh almost of content when Bison Billiam, with the coffee, passed him a great fat cigar. Charles-Norton threw a surreptitious glance at the heavy band; it was a dollar cigar.

Life, after all, has its compensations.

CHAPTER XVIII

And now, how about Charles-Norton and Dolly?

Well, they are getting along very well; very well, very well indeed.

Of course, they have their little differences—as have most couples. Mostly, it is about wings. There seems to be a something fundamental about both Charles-Norton and Dolly which irresistibly makes them diverge on the question of the proper length of wings (male wings at least). For a time, in fact, during the first months of their intoxicating public success and before they had arrived to the present adjustment, the question threatened to bring the conjugal craft to a final wreck. Strangely enough (or naturally enough) it is a catastrophe that eased the situation. One night, after Dolly, in a sudden access of resentment, had taken an immoderate whack out of the left wing, Charles-Norton tumbled to the ground in the midst of his performance, and broke his ankle.

It was, of course, in an agony of remorse that Dolly nursed her husband during his long month of enforced and bed-ridden idleness. Luckily, Bison Billiam behaved beautifully. He let the salary run on during the whole course of Charles-Norton's incapacity, and then, with genial inspiration, prevailed upon him, when he had recovered, to make his public reappearance with the heavy plaster-of-paris cast still upon the injured leg—which immensely increased the Flying Wonder's popularity and success.

A *modus vivendi* was agreed upon after this, which is still in force and works very well. Bison Billiam was made the permanent arbitrator of the wing question. Whenever they have a little difference now, Charles-Norton and Dolly go to Bison Billiam, and, standing before him hand in hand, listen to a sage adjudication of their rights and their wrongs. They call him Papa Bison.

And so, they are quite happy. Dolly, of course, takes a keen pleasure in her home. She has a neat little brick house, with a white door, near the Riverside Drive, and a butler. A butler always had been Dolly's secret dream.

Charles-Norton, also, though unconsciously perhaps, gets a good deal of pleasure out of the house (and the butler), for Dolly, with innate genius, has given it an air of quiet elegance and culture which he secretly enjoys. There is, also, a certain contentment in living life along a definite routine. He flies every night but Sunday, and two afternoons a week. And then, if Dolly has her house, he has his automobile.

A big, high-powered, red automobile. He goes out in it with Dolly every Sunday. When he arrives to a certain point in a certain highway, where the road is smooth and hard, and undulates up and down like a Coney Island chute for many miles, he leans forward and puts his chin close to the back of the chauffeur, who is French, and looks like Mephistopheles.

"Let her out," he says.

The chauffeur, with a grin, "lets her out"—and they swoop down and up, down and up, in increasing speed. The road is a ribbon, which she rolls hungrily within her; the trees, the rare houses on both sides, coalesce into two solid, whirling walls.

"Faster," says Charles-Norton.

The world becomes two parallel planes of solid atmosphere, rushing along close to right and left; the air strikes their faces like a fist, closing their nostrils till they gasp; the machine's hum becomes a cry; its flaps rise like wings.

"Faster," says Charles-Norton.

He seems to leave his body; it wafts off behind on a current of air, like a hat—and he is only a soul, a delicious kernel of soul ecstatically drunk, floating like an atom through the eternities.

"Faster," he says.

But he is aware now of a shrill, insistent, strident sound. It drills into his soul; it will not be quiet; it will not let him be. Bing! His body, catching up from behind, drops about him again—and then he knows. It is Dolly; Dolly screaming, poor little Dolly hysterical with fear.

"Slow up," he says to the chauffeur.

The world gradually changes from a mere blur of parallel lines to visible groupings of matter. Trees, houses, the road, the sky reappear as through a curtain torn before them. The chauffeur wipes his brow. "Ah, Monsieur!" he says.

And Dolly, very pale, says with an impatience that seems weary, as though it were repeating itself for the thousandth time "Oh, Goosie, why, why, why will you scare me so?"

Charles-Norton is penitent, but a bit morose. "Gee," he says; "that wasn't fast. That wasn't fast." His eyes go off, very far; a vague, vague yearning, covered over with layer and layer of resignation, palpitates faintly at the pit of his being. "You don't know what speeding is," he murmurs; "you don't know——"

The machine, at smooth half-speed, is returning toward the city. "I won't go with you again," says Dolly.

But she always does. She doesn't like to ride fast, and he does, but she never lets him ride alone. 'Cause she loves him!

He will have to be more careful now, however. The other evening, as they sat in the cozy reading-room (lined with editions de luxe) after the performance, she got upon his knee and, hiding his eyes with her hands so he could not look at her, whispered something in his ear.

Charles-Norton sat silent a long moment after that. Then he said, as though speaking to himself: "I wonder if *he* will—if *he* will also—if *he* will——"

"I wonder; I wonder!" said Dolly, ecstatically, her eyes wide upon a splendid vision.

"We could keep them down," said Charles-Norton, consideringly, "by beginning early. By beginning early, with bandages, we could keep them down——"

To his great amazement, Dolly dissented. "Oh, no, no, no, no!" she cried. "Oh, he would look so cute with them—just like a little angel! Just like a little angel, Goosie!"

And Charles-Norton is still wondering about this differentiation in Dolly's wise little head, wondering why *he* can, while Goosie—can't.

THE END

Milton Keynes UK
Ingram Content Group UK Ltd.
UKHW030743071024
449371UK00006B/610